Custom Wooden Boxes
for the Scroll Saw

by Diana Thompson

Fox
Chapel Publishing Co. Inc.
1970 Broad Street • East Petersburg, PA 17520 • www.foxchapelpublishing.com

Acknowledgments

Kind heavenly Father, thank you for all the undeserved blessings.

A special thanks to "Captain" for all his encouragement and unconditional backing.

Thank you, Ayleen Stellhorn—you're the best editor an author could have.

A special thanks to Rick Hutcheson, my unfailing scroll saw guru! You've never let me down!

Thank you to all "my people," who have been so receptive to my work and helped to make it such a success. Bless you all.

Publisher	Alan Giagnocavo
Book Editor	Ayleen Stellhorn
Editorial Assistant	Gretchen Bacon
Photography	Pam Baynard
Cover Design	Jon Deck
Desktop Specialist	Linda Eberly, Eberly Designs, Inc.

ISBN 1-56523-212-7

Library of Congress Preassigned Card Number: 2003116143

To order your copy of this book,
please send check or money order
for the cover price plus $3.50 shipping to:
Fox Chapel Publishing Co.
Book Orders
1970 Broad St.
East Petersburg, PA 17520

Or visit us on the web at **www.foxchapelpublishing.com**

Manufactured in Korea
10 9 8 7 6 5 4 3 2 1

Because scrolling wood and other materials inherently includes the risk of injury and damage, this book cannot guarantee that creating the projects in this book is safe for everyone. For this reason, this book is sold without warranties or guaranties of any kind, expressed or implied, and the publisher and author disclaim any liability for any injuries, losses or damages caused in any way by the content of this book or the reader's use of the tools needed to complete the projects presented here. The publisher and the author urge all scrollers to thoroughly review each project and to understand the use of all tools before beginning any project.

Table of Contents

Dear "My People,"

I think of those who use my work as "my people," and that means that I think of all of you as mine! And y'all are the very best part of my work. Thanks to each one of you for hanging in there with me as I've grown in this artform and hopefully improved upon my first efforts. If it weren't for all of you who have been so accepting of my work, there wouldn't be this fifth book!

This book is going to be a bit different from all of the others. We're off on a new adventure—making wooden keepsake boxes. The method came about quite by accident. I was dinking around on the computer one day, just doodling with my drawing program. One design looked like a small gift box, so I made it. Then I realized it didn't have to be so small nor any particular shape. One thing led to another, one idea led to another, and the results are in this book. As always, the inspirations came from ordinary things we see every day. If y'all come up with some new ideas that would make good boxes, please pass them along. I'm always open to suggestions!

Of course, a book by me wouldn't be complete without a few compound patterns included. This method of sawing comes into its own when designing the box handles.

Once this book is in the hands of my so talented, patient and long-suffering editor, Ayleen Stellhorn (without whom, I'd be lost), my next plans are to do a box of each state, with the state flower done in the compound sawing method on the lids. Wish me luck!

Best regards,
Diana Thompson

ABOUT THE AUTHOR

Still a resident of her much-loved Mobile, Alabama, Diana Thompson is an avid scroller and designer, focusing especially on compound cutting. She began scrolling several years ago when she experimented on her husband's old scroll saw while he was at work. Since then, she has written four books on compound designs, and her husband, Bob, has bought five scroll saws just for her. This book features Diana's compound designs and her innovative wooden boxes that can be made entirely on the scroll saw. When she's not scrolling, Diana finds time to escape to the golf course. You can see more of her work online at www.scrollsawinspirations.com.

BOX MAKING BASICS

First and foremost, keep your safety in mind at all times. Consider the following safety precautions before you begin.

- Always wear some type of eye protection.
- Use a dust mask to protect your respiratory system, as some woods are irritants and can cause health problems.
- Never wear loose fitting clothing around moving machinery. It can easily get caught in moving parts and cause injury.
- Carefully read the manufacturer's instructions and take the appropriate

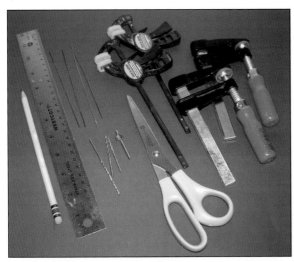

General tools for box-making include a pencil, ruler, assorted scroll saw blades and drill bits, scissors and various clamps.

Tools to make boxes

- Scroll saw
- Saw blades #5, 5R, and #7
- Wood of choice
- Drill and assorted bits
- Assorted clamps of choice
- ⅛" round over router bit (optional)
- Scissors
- Pencil
- Ruler
- Rotary tool with router table attachment (optional)
- Rotary tool mounted in drill press attachment
- Spray adhesive
- Clear packing tape
- ¾" cellophane tape
- Wood glue
- Assorted sandpaper grits

precautions before using any instrument or product.

An overview

Making boxes is a rather simple process once you have the basic ideas firmly planted in your head. There are several steps to creating a box on the scroll saw. I'll explain them briefly here, then demonstrate the technique later in the book.

Gather the wood and cut it to a manageable size. As you'll see later, I don't always start with a square piece of wood. Sometimes I lop off an odd shaped end of a board or cut a rough circular-shaped piece. A smaller piece of wood is easier to use on the scroll saw than a larger piece.

Glue the patterns to the wood. Always glue the pattern to the best side of the wood. The glue that holds the pattern in place can be removed with mineral spirits or acetone.

Cut the inside line of the box sides first. This forms the hole inside the box.

Glue the box bottom to the wood for the box sides, then cut the outside line of the box sides. This forms the outside edge of the box and the bottom in one step and ensures that both are even. This is a better method than cutting the sides and

the bottom separately, then gluing them together: You would never get a perfect match. Set the assembled bottom of the box aside.

If there is any fretwork or other decorative saw work on the lid, cut that now. This includes inlay and relief work, as well as fretwork. Set this piece aside.

Cut the inside line of the underside of the lid next. This will form the lip that overlaps the top outside edge of the box.

Glue the lip to the wood for the box top, then cut the outside line. The top of the box is now finished. Rout the edges for a nice finish, then finish the box as desired.

Wood choice

Before you start cutting boxes, take time to pick out your favorite woods. If you're new to scrolling and are unsure of what type of wood to choose, try using basswood, white pine, sugar pine or any of

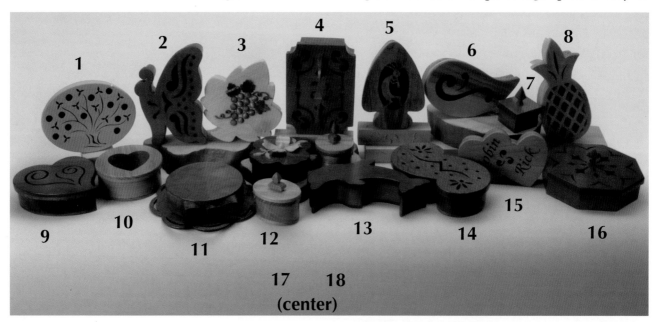

A variety of woods were used to create the boxes in this book. This photo shows a sampling of my favorites. (Note: Some boxes use woods different from those shown in the pattern section.)

1 Yellow Cedar (Tree of Life Box. Pattern on page 43.)
2 Spanish Cedar (Butterfly Box. Pattern on page 69.)
3 Poplar (Grape Leaf Box. Pattern on page 95.)
4 Redwood (Dreams Box. Pattern on page 6.)
5 Canary Wood (Kokopelli Box. Pattern on page 49.)
6 Willow (Teardrop Box. Pattern on page 55.)
7 Red Cedar (Tiny Diamond Box. Pattern on page 25.)
8 Aspen (Pineapple Welcome Box. Pattern on page 46.)
9 Narra (Whimsical Heart Box. Pattern on page 52.)
10 Cyprus with Black Walnut (Classic Round Box with Heart Inlay. Pattern on page 103.)

11 Sugar Pine and Birch Plywood (Bonnet Box. Pattern on page 40.)
12 Cyprus (Tiny Oval Box. Pattern on page 25.)
13 Redwood (Dolphin Box. Pattern on page 38.)
14 Lacewood (Scroll Box. Pattern on page 85.)
15 Alder (Double Heart Box. Pattern on page 92.)
16 Genuine Mahogany (Kaleidoscope Box. Pattern on page 77.)
17 Black Walnut with Magnolia (Dogwood Box. Pattern on page 98.)
18 Butternut (Tiny Round Box. Pattern on page 25.)

the cedars. All of the cedars are a pleasure to work with and finish nicely. Also keep in mind that the softer the wood, the easier it is to cut.

All of the box patterns call for 1¼"-thick material; however, I have used thicker and thinner woods. The choice depends on the density of the wood and your particular saw.

The box lids and bottoms can be made using ¼"-thick wood. For many boxes, I will use identical wood for the sides and the lids. Others look nice with contrasting wood. Plywood is my wood of choice for the lids that I plan to paint. When making the lids from plywood, apply both pattern pieces to the "good side" of the plywood. This ensures the good side will show where it counts. Birch plywood works very well for the lids and box bottoms. It finishes easily and looks great. It also takes stain quite well.

Blades and saws

Any scroll saw will cut the patterns in this book, as long as the saw is in proper working order. Check your individual owner's manual for recommended maintenance.

Because the box sides are quite thick, I've found that using a #7 single tooth blade works best for cutting them. For the lids, I use a #5 or #5R (reverse tooth) blade. The reverse tooth blade eliminates a lot of the sanding, as it cuts smoother with little or no tear-out on the bottom side of wood. However, blade selection is generally a matter of personal choice, so don't be afraid to use your favorites or to experiment with different blade sizes.

When cutting the thicker or denser wood, such as that used on the box sides, it helps to apply clear packing tape to the wood. Be sure to put the packing tape on before applying the pattern. The shop lights cause a terrible glare on the tape, making it difficult to see the pattern lines if the tape is not applied first. The packing tape can also help you to avoid burning the wood as you're sawing.

On occasion, you may find that a bandsaw will be easier to use than a scroll saw when it comes to cutting the sides. This tip only works on the simpler boxes, such as the larger square or rectangular boxes. The bandsaw blade is not flexible enough to cut around the more complex animal or flower shapes.

When cutting the frets or letters in the lids, try backing the piece with some scrap ¼" stock. The underside will be much smoother, and the piece will be easier to control, especially if the stock is thin. There are several ways to hold two pieces of

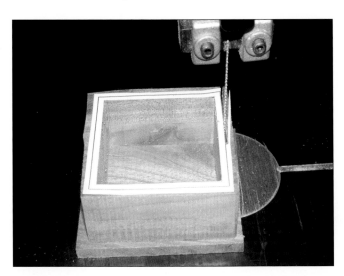

The outside lines of some of the simple boxes, such as the square box pictured here, can be cut on a bandsaw using a 1/8″ blade.

A rotary tool fitted into a router table attachment is used to round over the edges of the boxes.

wood together: run masking tape around them, place double sided tape between them, nail them together with tiny ½" wire brads (nails), or glue them together with hot glue. You can even try spraying both sides of a piece of paper with spray adhesive, then sandwiching that piece of paper between the two boards. Add pressure-sensitive two-sided tape, the same tape used for regripping golf clubs.

Finishing techniques

Most hardwoods are too beautiful to cover up with paint or stain. Keeping that in mind, I've finished all of the hardwood boxes in this book with a natural finish. Simply choose a water-based or a solvent-based wood sealer. Both are easy and quick to apply, though the water-based wood sealers tend to raise the grain a bit more, which requires some additional sanding.

General supplies for box-making include sandpaper of various grits, wood glue, repositionable adhesive spray, packing tape and scotch tape.

Not all of the boxes in this book are cut from hardwoods. Some are cut from pine or plywood and then painted. You can use any acrylic paint to paint your boxes in any number of ways. Simply apply a wood sealer first, sand, then paint. I don't consider myself a painter, so I've chosen to use simple blocked-in colors (see the Sunbonnet Sue Box on page 100) and sponge painting techniques. I imagine decorative tole painting would also look very nice on the lids and sides of a box.

Flocking is a simple technique that gives the insides of the box a nice, professional finish. It has a suede-like feel when it's dry. There are several different brands of flocking on the market. You'll want to experiment until you've found your favorite. Apply flocking after the final clear finish has been allowed to dry.

Experiment with finishing techniques from other crafts as well. I learned to decoupage one afternoon while watching television and decided to try it on a finished box. The result was beautiful.

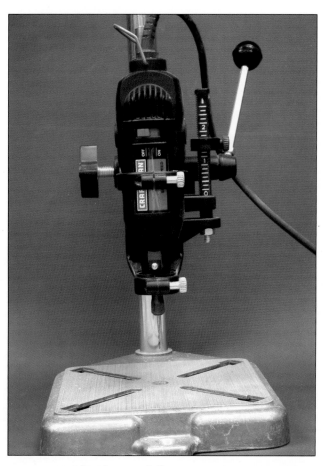

A rotary tool fitted into a drill press attachment is used to create starter holes for fretwork.

Making a DREAMS JEWELRY BOX

This beautiful box, cut from walnut, makes a perfect jewelry or trinket box. From a scroller's perspective, it combines a number of techniques: a fretwork lid, a compound handle, and built-in inside compartments. From a non-scroller's perspective, the overall effect is a stunning and treasured gift.

To make this box you will need five pieces of walnut of the following dimensions: 7" x 5" x 1¼" for the sides; 7" x 5" x ¼" for the bottom; 8" x 6" x ¼" for the lid top; 8" x 6" x ¼" for the lip of the lid; and 6" x 1½" x ¾" for the handle. Walnut is a beautiful wood, but it can be very difficult to cut on a scroll saw. Be sure to cut slowly, but not so slow that you burn the wood. You may want to try adding a layer of packing tape to the top of the piece. It seems that the scroll saw melts the tape just a fraction as it cuts and, in doing so, lubricates the blade.

As you work your way through the demonstration on the following pages, you will see that every box in this book can be created using the same method. This method encompasses four basic steps.

Cut the inside lines of the Box Side pattern from a thick piece of wood to create the sides of the box.

Glue a thin piece of wood to the bottom of the sides, then cut the outside lines of the Box Side pattern to form the outside edges of the box. Set this piece aside.

If the box has a fretwork lid, cut the frets now. If not, move directly to cutting the inside line of the Lid Underside pattern to form the lip of the box.

Glue a ¼" piece of wood to the lip of the box, then cut the outside lines of the Lid Underside pattern to form the outside edges of the lid.

"Dreams Box"

Lid assembly
After cutting out both lid sections,
glue lid underside to lid upperside,
with pattern sides facing out.
Clamp into place and allow to dry.
Cut out around the center line of
the lid underside, cutting through both
thicknesses.

Lid upperside
1/4" stock
Apply the pattern to the stock.
Cut around the outside line.
Cut out all frets.

#7 blade for cutting box sides
#5R blades for cutting lid
#5 blade for cutting handle

After box is assembled, before handle is glued
into place, round over lower
box edge and upper and lower lid edges
with a rotary tool fitted with a 1/8"
round over bit, or by hand with sandpaper.

Lid upperside

Handle
Cut according to 3-D directions
Glue to center of lid.

Dreams Jewelry Box Pattern

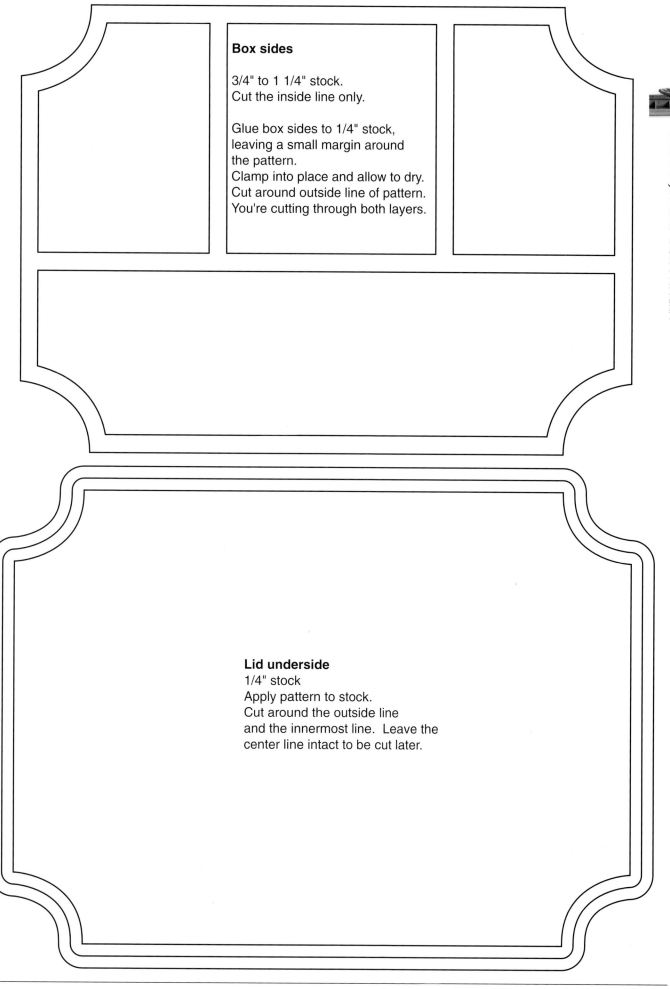

Box sides

3/4" to 1 1/4" stock.
Cut the inside line only.

Glue box sides to 1/4" stock,
leaving a small margin around
the pattern.
Clamp into place and allow to dry.
Cut around outside line of pattern.
You're cutting through both layers.

Lid underside
1/4" stock
Apply pattern to stock.
Cut around the outside line
and the innermost line. Leave the
center line intact to be cut later.

Cutting the "Dreams" Jewelry Box

1 Glue the Box Side pattern to the block. Cut all of the inside lines. These cuts will form the inside of the box and the compartments within.

2 Turn the block over; then, use a piece of folded sandpaper to smooth the inside edges of the box.

3 A block sander is used to smooth the bottom of the block.

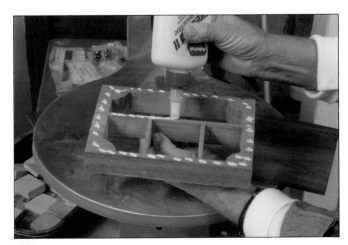

4 Apply wood glue to the sanded surface. Using closely positioned dots ensures that you apply the glue sparingly.

5 Spread the glue across the bottom of the cut block with your finger.

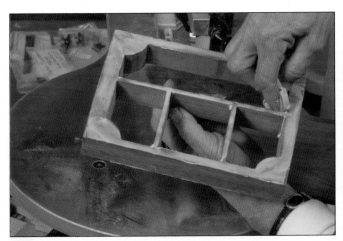

6 Wipe away any excess glue with a shop rag.

DREAMS JEWELRY BOX

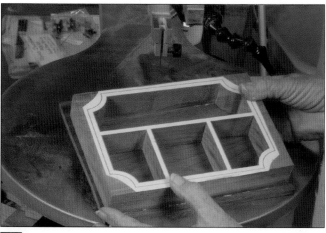

7 Turn the block back over and glue this piece to the ¼" piece of wood.

8 Clamp the two pieces of wood together until the glue is dry.

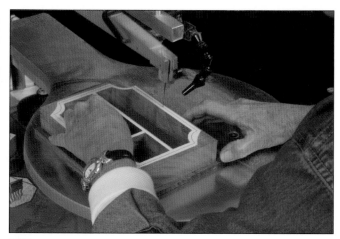

9 When the glue is dry, cut the outside lines of the Box Side pattern. This cut will, in effect, trim the sides of the box and the bottom of the box at the same time.

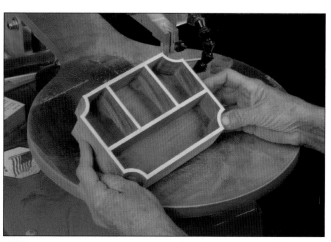

10 The bottom and sides of the box are now finished. Set it aside.

11 Apply the Lid Upperside pattern to the ¼" piece of wood; then, begin cutting the interior fretwork. Start with the comma shapes in any of the outside corners.

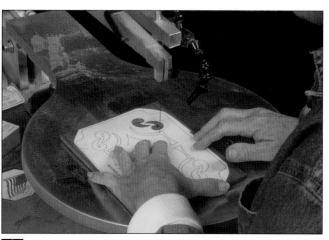

12 Next cut the "L" shapes just below the corners of the lid.

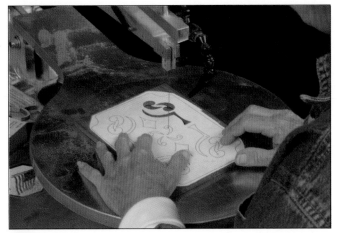

13 Cut the comma shapes at the center of the design next.

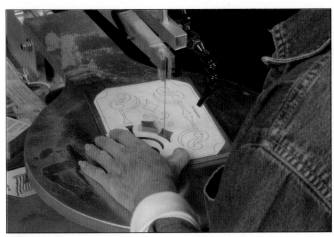

14 Cut the diamond shapes last. Note: This is a suggested progression. Altering this sequence will not compromise the strength of the wood.

15 All frets are cut out.

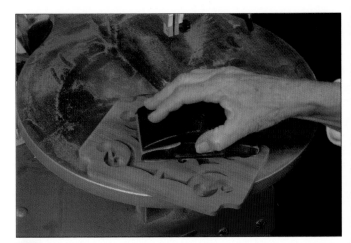

16 Turn the piece over and sand the underside of the lid with a sanding block to remove any burrs.

DREAMS JEWELRY BOX

17 Turn the piece back over and cut the outside line of the pattern. Set the trimmed piece aside.

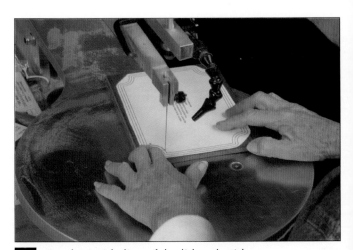

18 Cut the inside line of the lid underside.

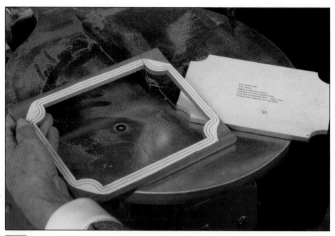

19 The Lid Underside pattern now looks like this. Discard (or save for future use) the wood from the center of the pattern.

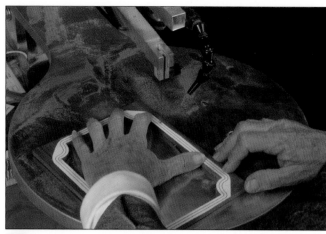

20 Cut the outside line of the Lid Underside pattern.

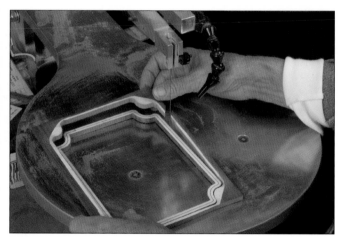

21 Remove the outside piece and discard it. The portion that is left will form the lip on the underside of the lid.

22 Turn the piece over and use a sanding block to sand away any burrs.

23 Apply wood glue to the sanded surface.

24 Glue the underside portion of the lid to the fretwork upperside, which was cut and set aside previously.

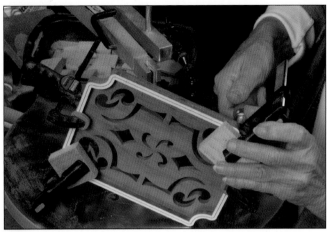

25 Clamp the pieces together until the glue is dry. Set aside.

26 Apply the Handle pattern to the ¾" deep x 1½" wide piece of wood as shown. Make sure the dotted line folds perfectly over one of the right angles of the block.

27 Clamp two pieces of waste wood to the sides of the block; then, begin by cutting the narrow side of the block first.

28 Remove the block from the clamps; then, tape the block together so that the handle will not shift within the block.

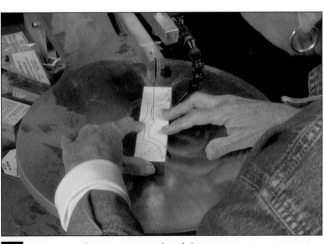

29 Now cut the opposite side of the pattern.

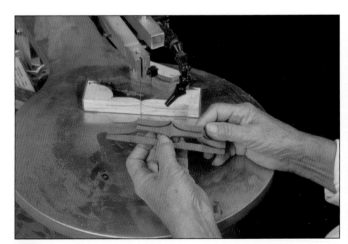

30 Carefully remove the pieces of wood to free the compound handle. Set the handle aside.

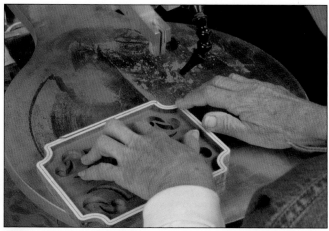

31 Remove the clamps from the lid and cut the remaining outside line of the Lid Underside pattern. This cut will, in effect, shape the outer edge of the lid and the lip at the same time.

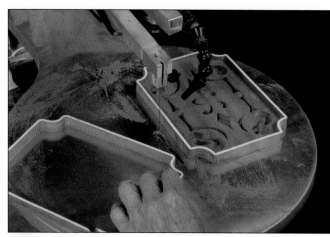

32 The lid of the box is now finished.

33 Remove the pattern from the top of the lid. Mineral spirits will loosen any stubborn pattern pieces.

34 The finished box pieces—lid, box and handle—are ready for assembly. Finish each separately with a spray-on or rub-on finish of your choice; then, glue the handle to the box. Note: The hard edges of the box and the lid can be routed prior to finishing, if you so desire. (See Chapter One.)

Cutting a SWAN MUSIC BOX

Turning any box into a music box is a relatively simple exercise. The addition of a second tier allows the compound cut figure to turn on the base. A purchased musical movement and turntable complete the assembly.

Any number of compound cut figures can top a music box. For those who are new to compound cutting, it is simply making two cuts on the same working stock to achieve a three-dimensional figure. The pattern consists of two sides: the front view and the profile view. The left side is cut first; then cut the right side. For such a simple concept, compound cutting turns out some fantastic figures that look much more complicated than they are.

I like to use a #5 skip or single tooth blade for compound cutting. The blade is flexible enough to make the intricate turns and curves. I don't recommend a reverse tooth blade because it has a tendency to slow the saw action down. Ultimately, the choice is yours, and it's perfectly okay to use your favorites.

The steps for cutting the swan music box topper will show you the easiest and quickest method to cut compound figures. The same techniques can be used for other music box toppers or for box handles.

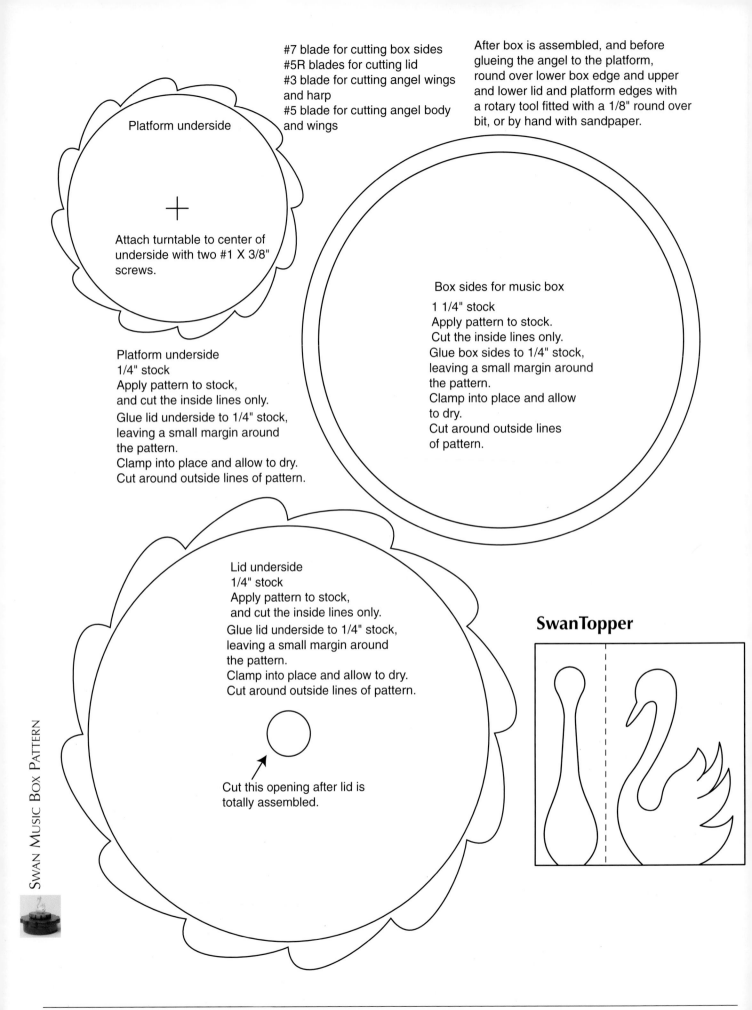

Platform underside

#7 blade for cutting box sides
#5R blades for cutting lid
#3 blade for cutting angel wings
and harp
#5 blade for cutting angel body
and wings

After box is assembled, and before
glueing the angel to the platform,
round over lower box edge and upper
and lower lid and platform edges with
a rotary tool fitted with a 1/8" round over
bit, or by hand with sandpaper.

Attach turntable to center of
underside with two #1 X 3/8"
screws.

Box sides for music box

1 1/4" stock
Apply pattern to stock.
Cut the inside lines only.
Glue box sides to 1/4" stock,
leaving a small margin around
the pattern.
Clamp into place and allow
to dry.
Cut around outside lines
of pattern.

Platform underside
1/4" stock
Apply pattern to stock,
and cut the inside lines only.
Glue lid underside to 1/4" stock,
leaving a small margin around
the pattern.
Clamp into place and allow to dry.
Cut around outside lines of pattern.

Lid underside
1/4" stock
Apply pattern to stock,
and cut the inside lines only.
Glue lid underside to 1/4" stock,
leaving a small margin around
the pattern.
Clamp into place and allow to dry.
Cut around outside lines of pattern.

SwanTopper

Cut this opening after lid is
totally assembled.

SWAN MUSIC BOX PATTERN

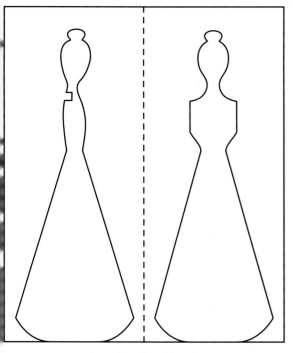

Angel body   Cut 1

#5 blade for angel's body and wings
#3 blade her arms and harp. Glue wings
into notch on body. Glue arms to sides of
body. Glue harp in hands.

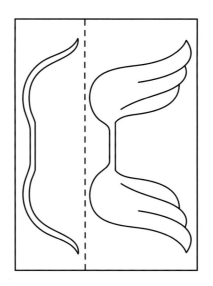

Angel wings   Cut 1

Harp Cut 1

1/8" stock
#3 blade
3/64 drill bit
Use a backer board
when cutting thin stock.

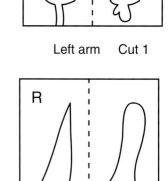

Left arm   Cut 1

R

Right arm   Cut 1

Angel Topper

Carousel Topper

Fold this section
over top of stock.

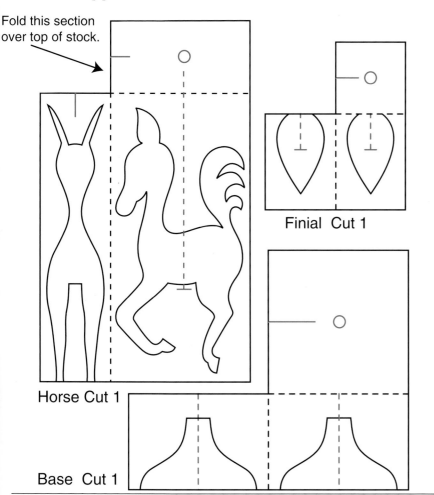

Horse Cut 1

Finial Cut 1

Base Cut 1

Male Swan Topper

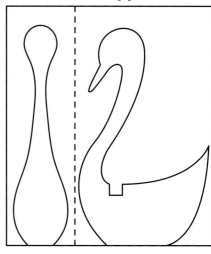

Male swan body Cut 1

Male swan wings Cut 1
Glue into notch on back of swan's back.

Cutting the Swan Music Box

1 Glue the Box Sides pattern to a block of wood about 4¼" x 4½" x exactly 1¼". Note: I cut a roughly circular piece of wood from a rather large board of mahogany, but cutting a square piece of wood down to the pattern circle is fine, also.

2 Turn the piece over and sand any burrs from the bottom of the piece.

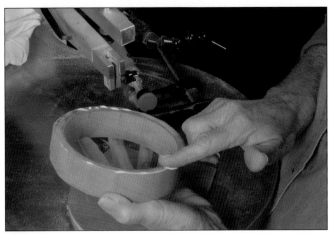

3 Apply dots of glue to the sanded surface and spread it around evenly with your finger.

4 Clamp the box sides to a piece of wood about 4½" x 4½" x exactly ¼". Set this piece aside and allow the glue to dry.

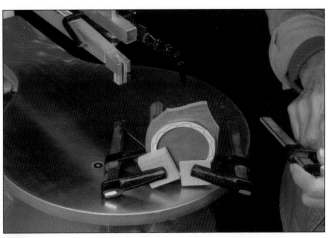

5 Set this piece aside and allow the glue to dry.

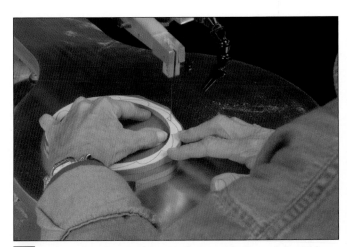

6 When the glue is dry, cut the outside line of the Lid Underside pattern. This cut will, in effect, shape the lip of the lid and the outside edge of the lid with one cut.

7 Remove the outer ring and discard it.

8 Place the inner portion of the pattern back into the recessed area on the underside of the lid.

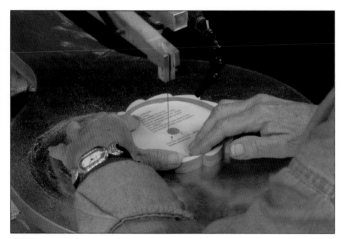

9 Cut the smaller circular opening in the center of the pattern.

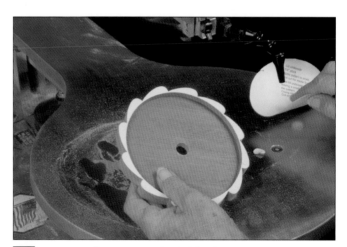

10 Remove the pattern. The lid for the music box will look like this.

11 Cut the turntable platform for the compound figure in the same manner. 1) Apply the Platform Underside pattern to a piece of wood about 3" x 3" x exactly ¼". 2) Cut the inside line. 3) Glue a second piece of wood about 3" x 3" x exactly ¼". 4) Cut the scalloped outside line.

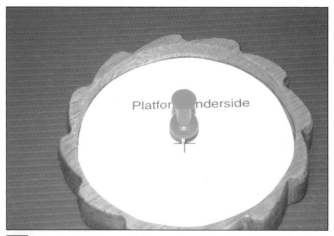

12 Mark the center of the underside with a thumbtack or pencil.

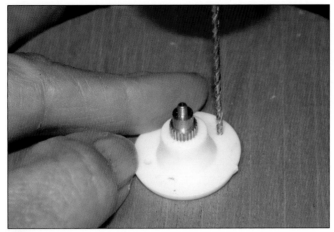

13 With a ¹⁄₁₆" drill bit, drill a hole on each side of the turntable.

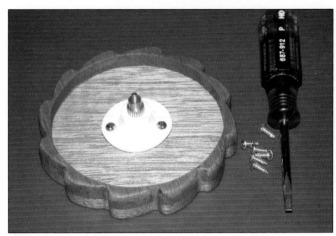

14 Use two-sided cellophane tape to hold the turntable in the center of the platform's underside; then attach the turntable with 2 #1 x ³⁄₈" screws.

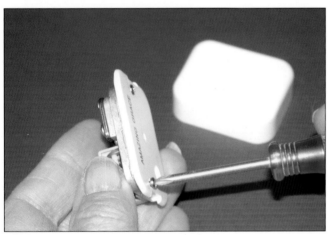

15 Remove the cover from the music mechanism. Remove the screws from the bottom and discard them or save them for another project.

16 Use two-sided cellophane tape to hold the mechanism in place on the underside of the lid. The shaft should be visible through the opening. Attach the mechanism with 2 #0 x ¹⁄₂" screws.

17 Fold the compound pattern for the swan over the block of wood. I am using a block of magnolia wood.

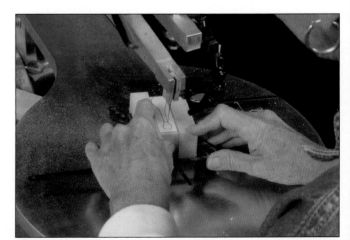

18 Clamp the block between two pieces of waste wood so it is easier to hold. Make the first cut on the narrow side of the block.

19 When the first cut is complete, remove the block from the clamp. Use a piece of cellophane tape to hold the cut piece securely in place inside the block.

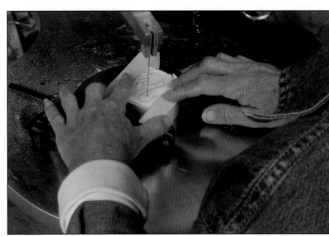

20 Once again, clamp the block between two pieces of waste wood. Cut the opposite side of the pattern.

21 Gently free the compound-cut swan from the block of wood. Use the finish of your choice to complete the swan; then, glue it to the top of the finished platform with wood glue.

TIPS

- Some compound patterns will have frets, or inside cuts. In this case, cut the frets first, starting with the left side of the pattern, then the right side. Smaller frets can be discarded; larger ones should be left in the block to give the figure stability and to hold it firmly in place.
- For the best results, cut to the waste side of the lines. Some compound patterns are quite delicate, and removing too much material will cause breakage.
- Blocks clamped to the figure help to keep the piece level while cutting, as well as keeping fingers a bit safer. Snug the clamps only tight enough to hold, but not so tight that they interfere with the blade moving through the kerf.

Music Box Supplies

Musical movement and turntable are available from:

National Artcraft
7996 Darrow Rd.
Twinsburg, OH 44087
888-937-2723
www.nationalartcraft.com
Stock #230-817-02 for movement,
Stock #231-505-01 for turntable

Making TINY BOXES

The question that crops up once you've made several boxes on your scroll saw is, "What do I do with all those left-over scraps of wood." Most of this wood, especially the wood that is cut away to create the box sides, is good, usable wood. And if you're like me and enjoy working with some of the more figured woods, those scraps are just worth too much money to throw them away.

The answer to the question about what to do with the scraps is simple: Use them to make miniature boxes.

Miniature boxes make excellent gifts for family and friends. They also make great practical items. A small diamond-shaped box placed on a windowsill near a sink is the perfect place to keep a diamond ring safe while working in the kitchen. A rectangular box placed on a dresser top is a good receptacle for loose pocket change at the end of the day.

In this chapter, you'll find five ideas for making smaller boxes from the waste wood of the larger projects. These are simple geometric boxes, including a circle box, an oval box, a square box, a rectangular box and a diamond box. The patterns for these boxes,

plus toppers that act as handles, can be found on the following pages. Follow the same basic method to cut these boxes. Once you have cut several, try cutting different shapes and adding different ornamentation. You'll be pleasantly surprised by these tiny gems!

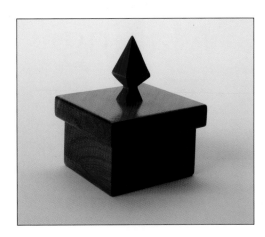

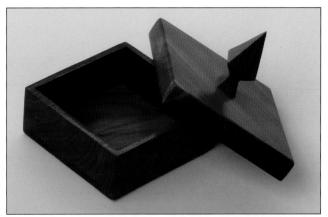

TINY BOXES

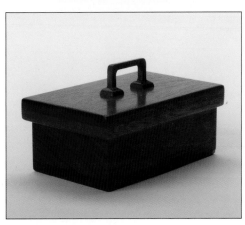

#7 blade for cutting box sides
#5R blades for cutting lid
#5 blade for cutting handle

After box is assembled, before handle is glued
into place, round over lower
box edge and upper and lower lid edges
with a rotary tool fitted with a 1/8"
round over bit, or by hand with sandpaper.

Diamond Box

Lid underside
1/4" stock
Apply pattern to stock,
and cut the inside lines only.
Glue lid underside to 1/4" stock,
leaving a small margin around
the pattern.
Clamp into place and allow to dry.
Cut around outside lines of pattern.

Oval Box

Lid underside
1/4" stock
Apply pattern to stock,
and cut the inside lines only.
Glue lid underside to 1/4" stock,
leaving a small margin around
the pattern.
Clamp into place and allow to dry.
Cut around outside lines of pattern.

Diamond Box

Box sides
3/4" to 1 1/4" stock.
Cut the inside line only.
Glue box sides to 1/4" stock,
leaving a small margin around
the pattern.
Clamp into place and allow to dry.
Cut around outside line of pattern.
You're cutting through both layers.

Oval Box

Box sides
3/4" to 1 1/4" stock.
Cut the inside line only.
Glue box sides to 1/4" stock,
leaving a small margin around
the pattern.
Clamp into place and allow to dry.
Cut around outside line of pattern.
You're cutting through both layers.

Square Box

Lid underside
1/4" stock
Apply pattern to stock,
and cut the inside lines only.

Glue lid underside to 1/4" stock,
leaving a small margin around
the pattern.
Clamp into place and allow to dry.
Cut around outside lines of pattern.

Square Box

Box sides
3/4" to 1 1/4" stock.
Cut the inside line only.
Glue box sides to 1/4" stock,
leaving a small margin around
the pattern.
Clamp into place and allow to dry.
Cut around outside line of pattern.
You're cutting through both layers.

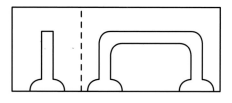

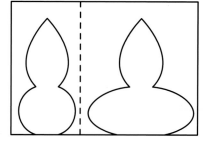

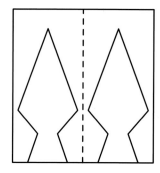

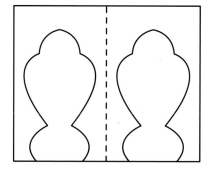

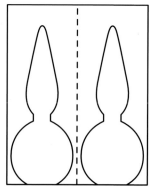

Handles
Cut according to 3-D directions.
Glue to center of box lids.

Rectangle Box

Lid underside
1/4" stock
Apply pattern to stock,
and cut the inside lines only.
Glue lid underside to 1/4" stock,
leaving a small margin around
the pattern.
Clamp into place and allow to dry.
Cut around outside lines of pattern.

Rectangle Box

Box sides
3/4" to 1 1/4" stock.
Cut the inside line only.
Glue box sides to 1/4" stock,
leaving a small margin around
the pattern.
Clamp into place and allow to dry.
Cut around outside line of pattern.
You're cutting through both layers.

Round Box
Lid underside
1/4" stock
Apply pattern to stock,
and cut the inside lines only.
Glue lid underside to 1/4" stock,
leaving a small margin around
the pattern.
Clamp into place and allow to dry.
Cut around outside lines of pattern.

Round Box
Box sides
3/4" to 1 1/4" stock.
Cut the inside line only.
Glue box sides to 1/4" stock,
leaving a small margin around
the pattern.
Clamp into place and allow to dry.
Cut around outside line of pattern.
You're cutting through both layers.

Making
CUSTOM
LIDS

Any handmade box is special, but a custom-made box is extra special. Any of the boxes in this book can be customized in several ways.

The first method, fretwork, is commonly used among scroll saw artists. In box-making, fretwork can be used to add a specific design or a name to the lid of a box. Try adding the company logo of a friend's business or a child's favorite storybook character. Create a pattern for a name by tracing the letters of the alphabet on to tracing paper or by using a computer program specifically designed to manipulate letters. You'll find one of my favorite alphabets on the following page as a starting point.

The second method, inlay, is well known but less commonly used among scrollers. To create an inlay lid requires that you tilt the saw table and cut through two stacked pieces of wood. An example of an inlay lid is shown beside the circle box below. In this chapter, I'll show you step-by-step how to

create an inlay lid and provide several patterns to get you started.

The third method, relief, is just gaining popularity among scrollers. Relief cutting involves tilting the saw table so that the cut piece either pushes forward or backward to create a raised or recessed design. Again, you'll find a step-by-step demonstration of the technique here, plus several patterns to try on your own.

Become familiar with all three of these techniques and the possibilities for creating custom boxes is endless. You will never want for a scroll saw idea again.

Relief

Relief cutting gives extra dimension to box lids. How far you tilt your saw will determine how highly raised your final design will be. A good starting number is 6½ degrees. I suggest cutting only in the direction shown here so that your final lid has a raised design. If you cut in the opposite direction, the design will be recessed—still a nice effect, but not quite as nice on a box lid as a raised design.

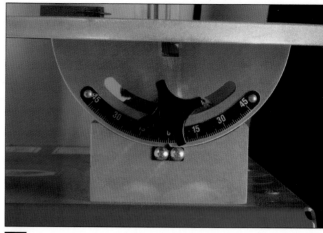

1 In order to do relief (and inlay) cutting, you will need to own a saw that has the option to tilt the saw table. This mechanism is located under the saw table.

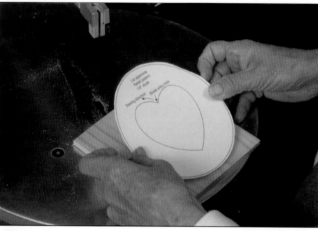

2 Position the pattern on the wood that you have chosen for the lid. Use temporary spray adhesive so the pattern can be easily removed after you are done sawing.

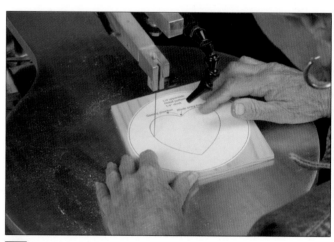

3 Make a very small starter hole in an inconspicuous spot along the cut line; then, begin cutting in the direction shown.

4 Gently push the center design up until it locks into place in the lid. I use watered down white glue just to be sure it stays in place.

CUSTOM LIDS

Reduce or enlarge to fit
the lid of your box, then
relief cut as explained
on the opposite page.

Inlay Lids

Inlay is not an exact science. Before beginning any inlay project, you should always complete a test piece. Use the pattern and the instructions below to test the settings on your saw before you begin to cut the lid.

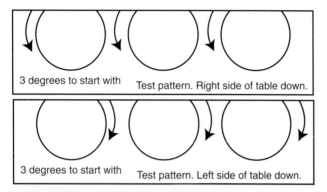

3 degrees to start with   Test pattern. Right side of table down.

3 degrees to start with   Test pattern. Left side of table down.

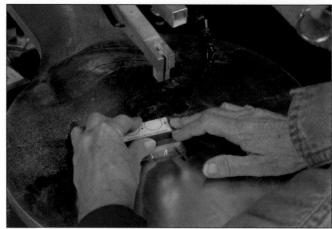

1 Stack two pieces of differently colored wood; then, tape the test pattern to the top with shipping tape. The color that you want to be inlaid should be on the top of the stack. Make sure both pieces are the same thickness.

2 Tilt the saw table to 3½ degrees, then cut in the direction shown. If the table is set correctly, the bottom fret should fall out, leaving the top fret to fall into place in the bottom piece of wood.

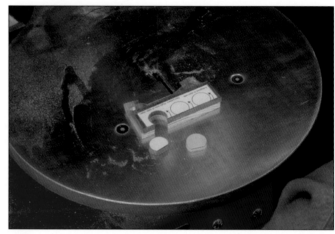

3 If the table is set incorrectly, both the bottom fret and the top fret will fall out of the wood. Reset your table and try again.

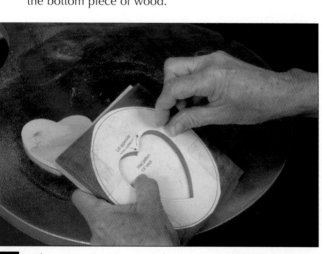

4 When your saw is correctly set, repeat the same steps above on the lid. 1) Stack two pieces of wood. 2) Use packing tape to hold the pattern and the two pieces of wood together. 3) Drill a very small starter hole in an inconspicuous spot along the cut line and begin cutting. 4) Remove the bottom piece, allowing the top piece to fall into position. 5) Finish the lid by cutting the lip and the outside pattern as shown in Steps 18-25 and Steps 31-34 on pages 10-13.

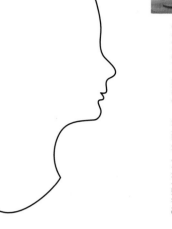

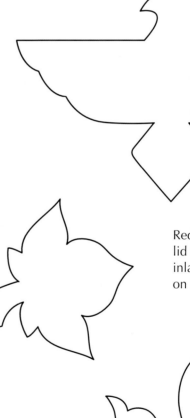

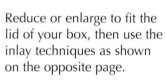

Reduce or enlarge to fit the lid of your box, then use the inlay techniques as shown on the opposite page.

Fretwork

Customizing and personalizing box lids is easy with fretwork techniques. Here I will show you how to use the alphabet on the opposite page to add names to a box lid. Any alphabet can be used, just be sure that you make accommodations for the scroll saw. Some script type faces will fall apart if you don't alter them before you make your cuts. The alphabet on the opposite page is "scroll saw ready" and is one of my favorites.

1 Using a light table or a window, trace the letters to the pattern. A line, which doesn't necessarily have to be straight, will guide you in placing the letters accurately.

2 Add each letter side-by-side, paying close attention to the spaces between the letters. Programs that manipulate type in just this manner are available for computer users.

3 The final pattern is ready to be cut.

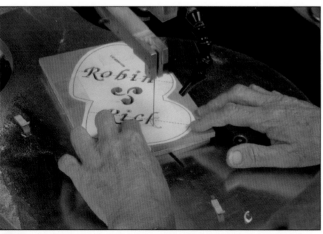

4 Cut the fretwork design carefully. Then proceed with finishing the box lid as instructed in Steps 15–25 on pages 10–12.

CUSTOM LIDS

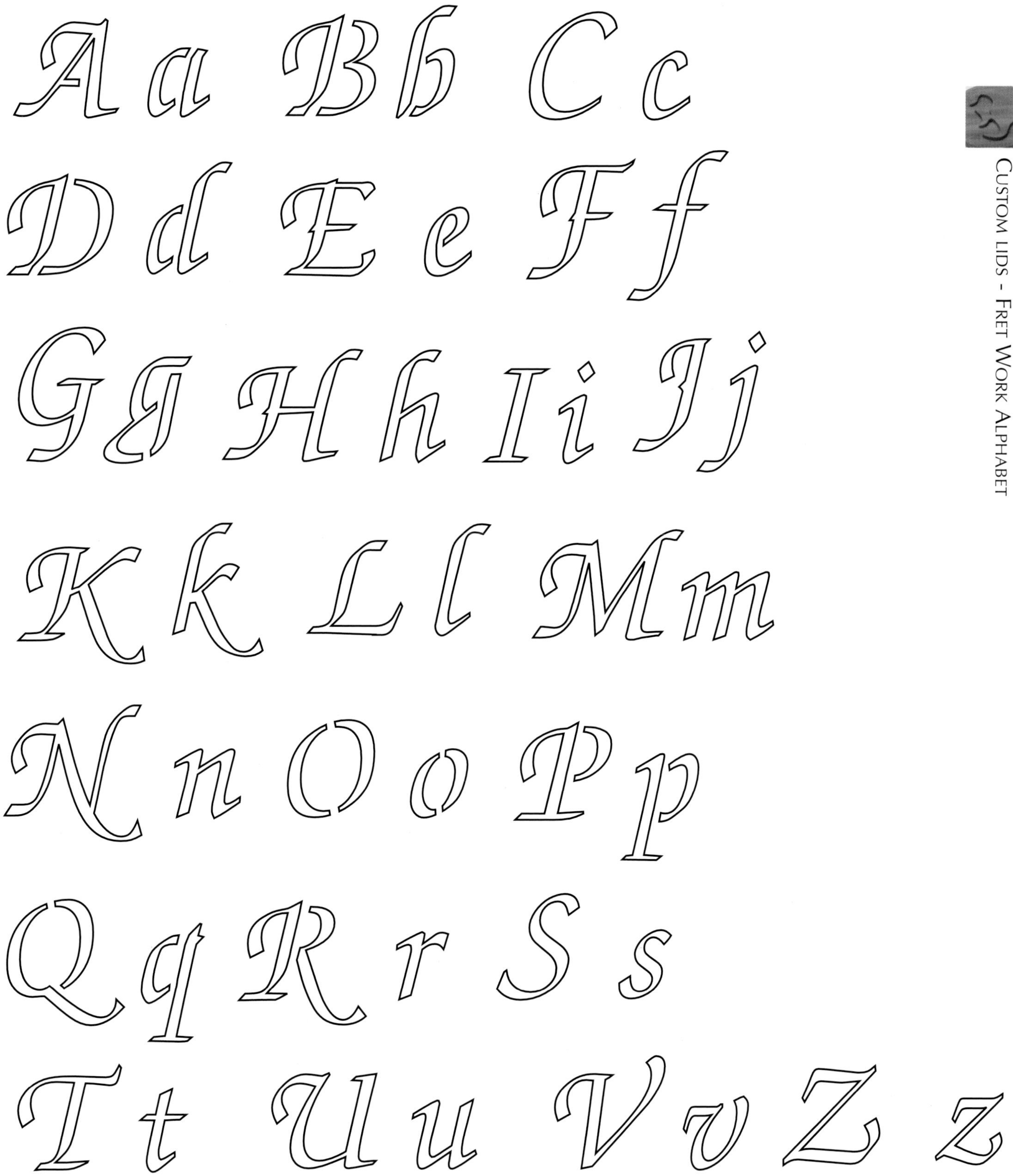

Aa Bb Cc
Dd Ee Ff
Gg Hh Ii Jj
Kk Ll Mm
Nn Oo Pp
Qq Rr Ss
Tt Uu Vv Zz
Ww Xx Yy

PENCIL BOX

Overall dimensions:
8¾" x 4" x 1½"

Wood: Canary Wood

This old-fashioned pencil box is a classic beauty. A long narrow compartment holds pens and pencils; smaller compartments hold paper clips, erasers or tacks.

Box sides
3/4" to 1 1/4" stock
#7 blade
Apply pattern to stock.
Cut the inside lines only.
Glue box sides to 1/4"
stock, leaving a small
margin around the
pattern. Clamp into
place and allow to dry.
Cut around outside
lines of pattern.

Lid underside
#5R blades for cutting lid
1/4" stock
Apply pattern to stock,
and cut the inside lines only.

Glue lid underside to 1/4" stock,
leaving a small margin around
the pattern.
Clamp into place and allow to dry.
Cut around outside lines of pattern.

After box is assembled, round over lower
box edge and upper and lower lid edges
with a rotary tool fitted with a 1/8"
round over bit, or by hand with sandpaper.

Helpful hint: If using plywood, be sure that
both lid patterns are adhered to the good
side. This insures the unfinished side of the
plywood will be glued together, leaving the
good side to show.

Swan Box

Overall dimensions:
    7¼ " x 5" x 1½"

Wood: Cypress

A highly figured grain will add interest to the delicate lines of this box. Position the pattern on the wood several ways before cutting for the best advantage.

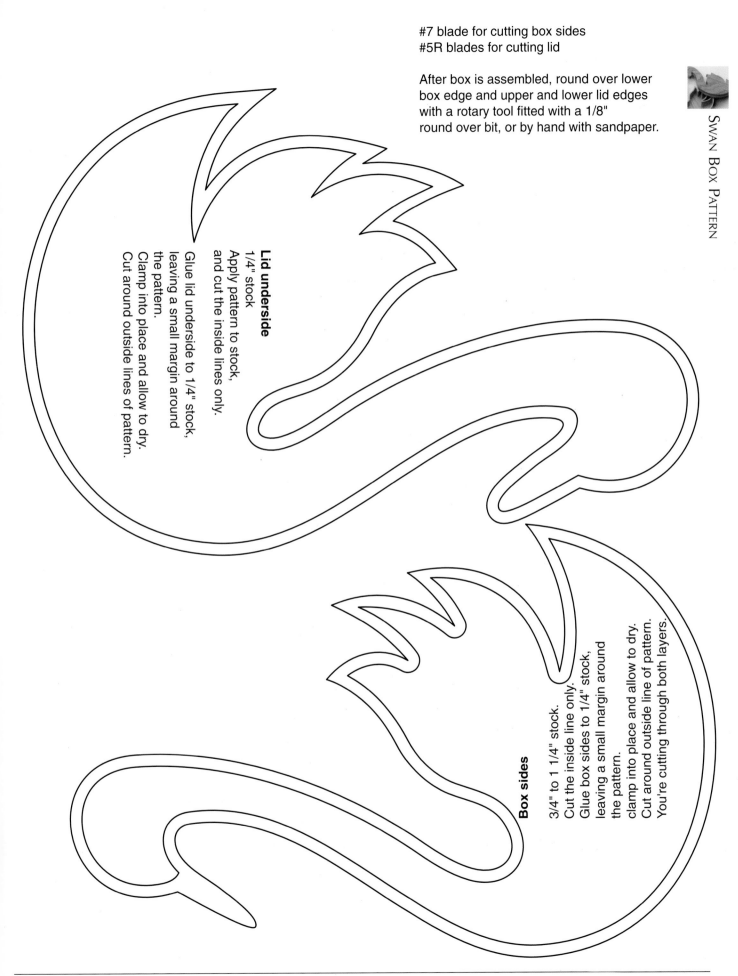

#7 blade for cutting box sides
#5R blades for cutting lid

After box is assembled, round over lower
box edge and upper and lower lid edges
with a rotary tool fitted with a 1/8"
round over bit, or by hand with sandpaper.

Lid underside
1/4" stock
Apply pattern to stock,
and cut the inside lines only.

Glue lid underside to 1/4" stock,
leaving a small margin around
the pattern.
Clamp into place and allow to dry.
Cut around outside lines of pattern.

Box sides

3/4" to 1 1/4" stock.
Cut the inside line only.
Glue box sides to 1/4" stock,
leaving a small margin around
the pattern.
clamp into place and allow to dry.
Cut around outside line of pattern.
You're cutting through both layers.

DOLPHIN BOX

Overall dimensions:
   7$\frac{1}{4}$" x 8$\frac{1}{4}$" x 1$\frac{1}{2}$"

Wood: Redwood

The layers of construction – bottom, sides, lip and top – are easily spotted on the side view of this box, but they do not detract from the box's sleek design.

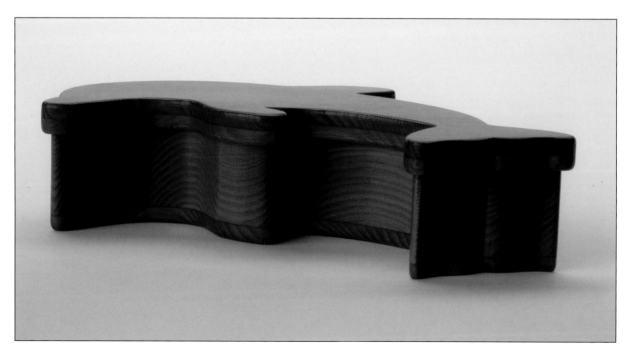

#7 blade for cutting box sides
#5R blades for cutting lid

After box is assembled, round over lower
box edge and upper and lower lid edges
with a rotary tool fitted with a 1/8"
round over bit, or by hand with sandpaper.

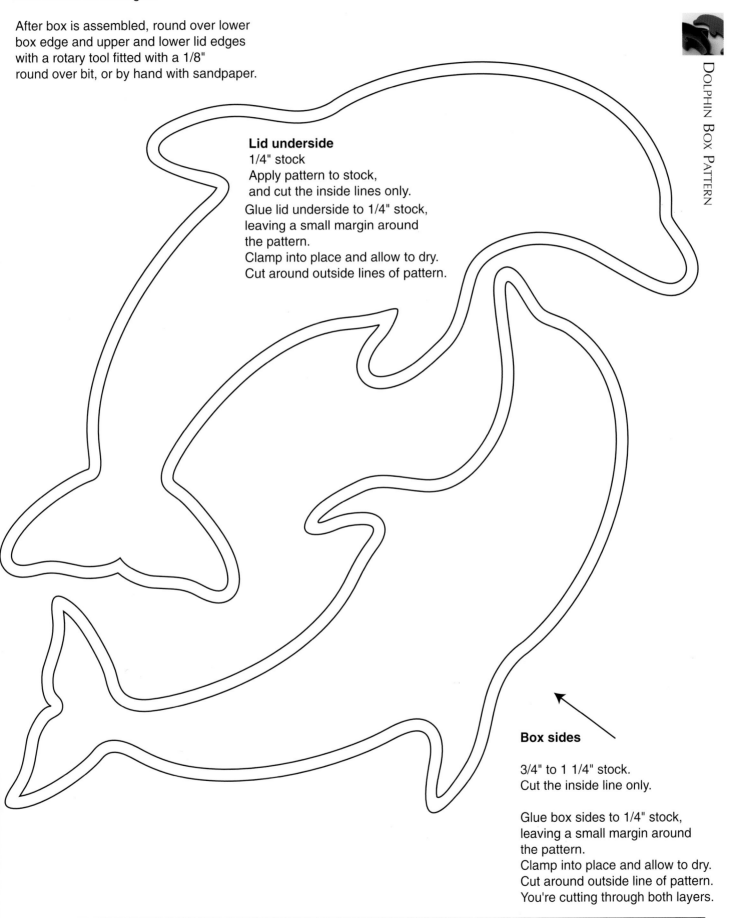

Lid underside
1/4" stock
Apply pattern to stock,
and cut the inside lines only.
Glue lid underside to 1/4" stock,
leaving a small margin around
the pattern.
Clamp into place and allow to dry.
Cut around outside lines of pattern.

Box sides

3/4" to 1 1/4" stock.
Cut the inside line only.

Glue box sides to 1/4" stock,
leaving a small margin around
the pattern.
Clamp into place and allow to dry.
Cut around outside line of pattern.
You're cutting through both layers.

BONNET BOX

Overall dimensions:
$7^3/_8$" x $7^3/_8$" x $1^1/_2$"

Wood: Sugar Pine and Birch plywood

A compound cut bow and a decorative base give this box the look of a lady's sun bonnet. Experiment with different combinations of wood for a different appearance.

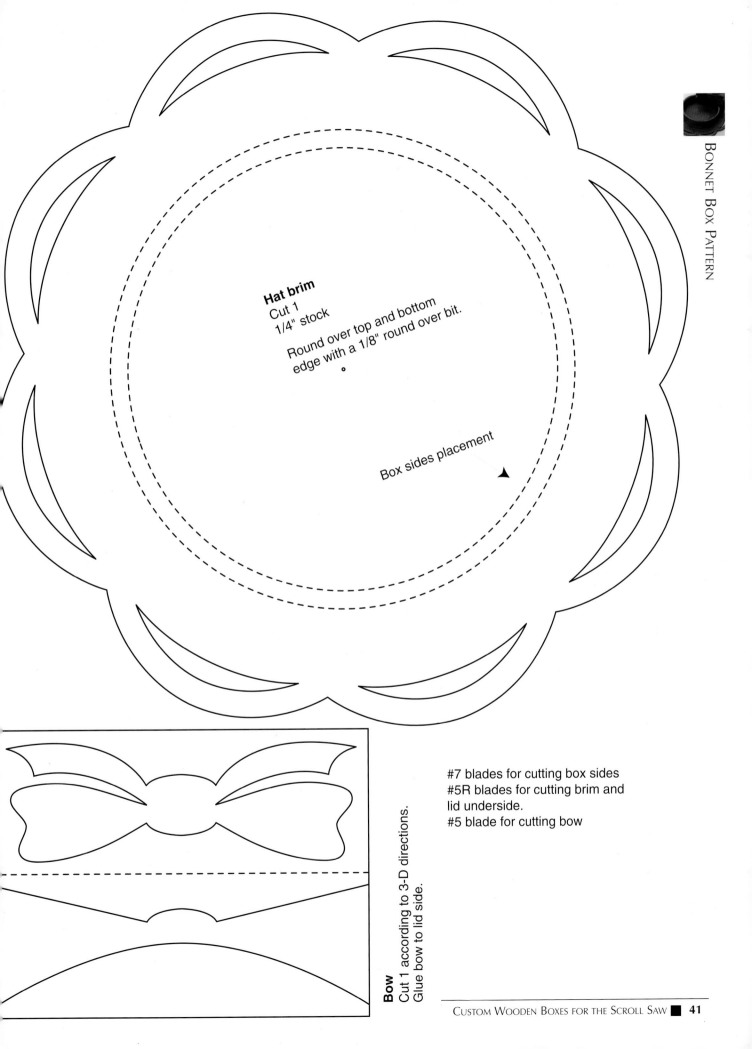

Hat brim
Cut 1
1/4" stock

Round over top and bottom
edge with a 1/8" round over bit.

Box sides placement

#7 blades for cutting box sides
#5R blades for cutting brim and
lid underside.
#5 blade for cutting bow

Bow
Cut 1 according to 3-D directions.
Glue bow to lid side.

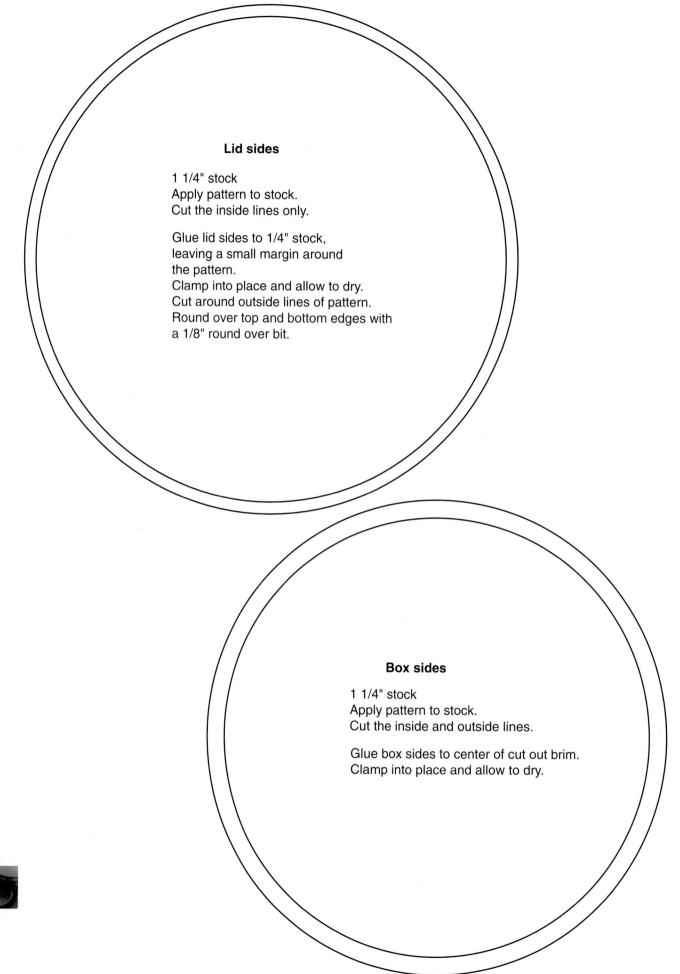

Lid sides

1 1/4" stock
Apply pattern to stock.
Cut the inside lines only.

Glue lid sides to 1/4" stock,
leaving a small margin around
the pattern.
Clamp into place and allow to dry.
Cut around outside lines of pattern.
Round over top and bottom edges with
a 1/8" round over bit.

Box sides

1 1/4" stock
Apply pattern to stock.
Cut the inside and outside lines.

Glue box sides to center of cut out brim.
Clamp into place and allow to dry.

TREE OF LIFE BOX

Overall dimensions:
6⁷/₈" x 5¹/₈" x 1¹/₂"

Wood: Yellow Cedar

A plain oval box is transformed into a special gift with a modern rendition of a folk art classic. Try designing your own fretwork pattern to fit within the dimensions of the lid.

#7 blade for cutting box sides
#5R blades for cutting lid
#3 or 3R for cutting frets
Round over edges with a rotary
tool fitted with a small round over bit,
or by hand with sandpaper.

Lid upperside
1/4" stock
Apply the pattern to the stock.
Cut around the outside line.
Cut out all frets.

Lid assembly
After cutting out both lid sections,
glue lid underside to lid top,
with pattern sides facing out.
Clamp into place and allow to dry.
Cut out around the center line of
the lid underside

Box sides

3/4" to 1 1/4" stock
Apply pattern to stock.
Cut the inside lines only.

Glue box sides to 1/4" stock,
leaving a small margin around
the pattern.
Clamp into place and allow to dry.
Cut around outside lines of pattern.

Lid underside
1/4" stock
Apply pattern to stock.
Cut around the outside line,
and the innermost line. Leave the
center line intact to be cut later.

PINEAPPLE BOX

Overall dimensions:
$8^{5}/8$" x $4^{1}/4$" x $1^{1}/2$"

Wood: Aspen

Long a symbol of welcome in Pennsylvania German households, the pineapple is also an excellent basis for a gift box. The lattice-work lid gives the recipient a quick look at the contents.

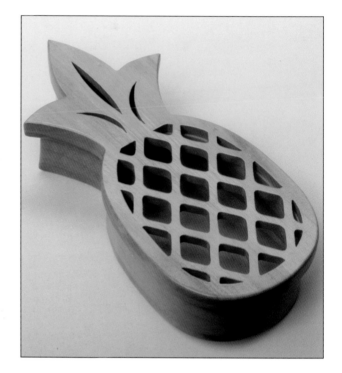

#7 blade for cutting box sides
#5R blades for cutting lid

After box is assembled, round over lower
box edge and upper and lower lid edges
with a rotary tool fitted with a 1/8"
round over bit, or by hand with sandpaper.

Lid assembly
After cutting out both lid sections,
glue lid underside to lid upperside,
with pattern sides facing out.
Clamp into place and allow to dry.
Cut out around the center line of
the lid underside, cutting through both
thicknesses.

Lid top
1/4" stock
Apply the pattern to the stock.
Cut around the outside line.
Cut out all frets.

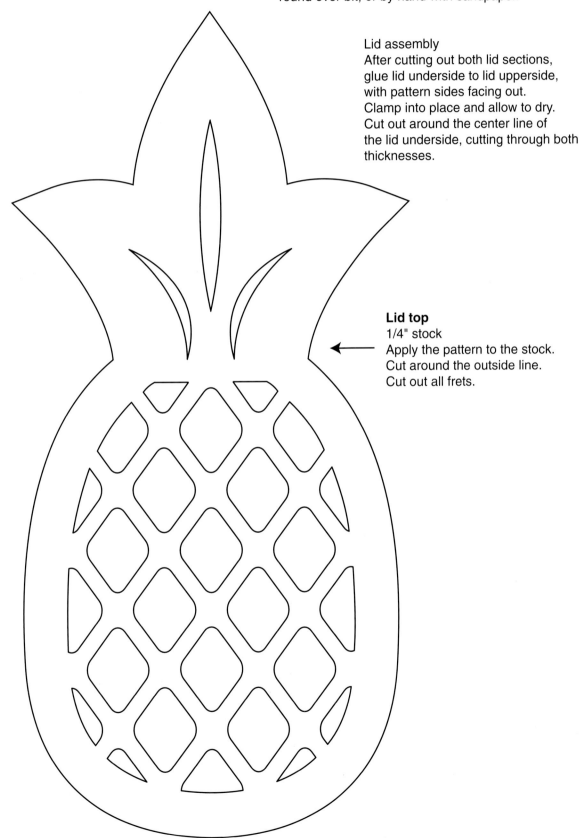

Box sides

3/4" to 1 1/4" stock.
Cut the inside line only.

Glue box sides to 1/4" stock,
leaving a small margin around
the pattern.
Clamp into place and allow to dry.
Cut around outside line of pattern.
You're cutting through both layers.

Lid underside
1/4" stock
Apply pattern to stock.
Cut around the outside line,
and the innermost line. Leave the
center line intact to be cut later.

KOKOPELLI BOX

Overall dimensions:
    6⁷/₈" x 5¹/₈" x 1¹/₂"

Wood: Canary Wood

Dark wood makes this traditional
Native American figure stand out from
the shadowed interior of the arrowhead-
shaped box.

#7 blade for cutting box sides
#5R blades for cutting lid
3/64 drill bit for pilot holes

After box & lid are assembled, round over
lower box edge and upper and lower lid
edges with a rotary tool fitted with a 1/8"
round over bit, or by hand with sandpaper.

Lid assembly
After cutting out both lid sections,
glue lid underside to lid upperside,
with pattern sides facing out.
Clamp into place and allow to dry.
Cut out around the center line of
the lid underside, cutting through both
thicknesses.

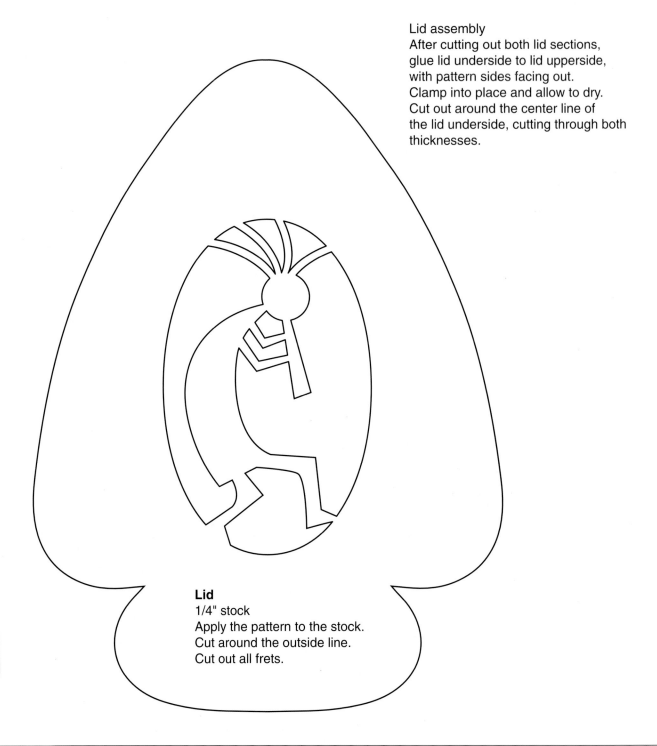

Lid
1/4" stock
Apply the pattern to the stock.
Cut around the outside line.
Cut out all frets.

KOKOPELLI BOX PATTERN

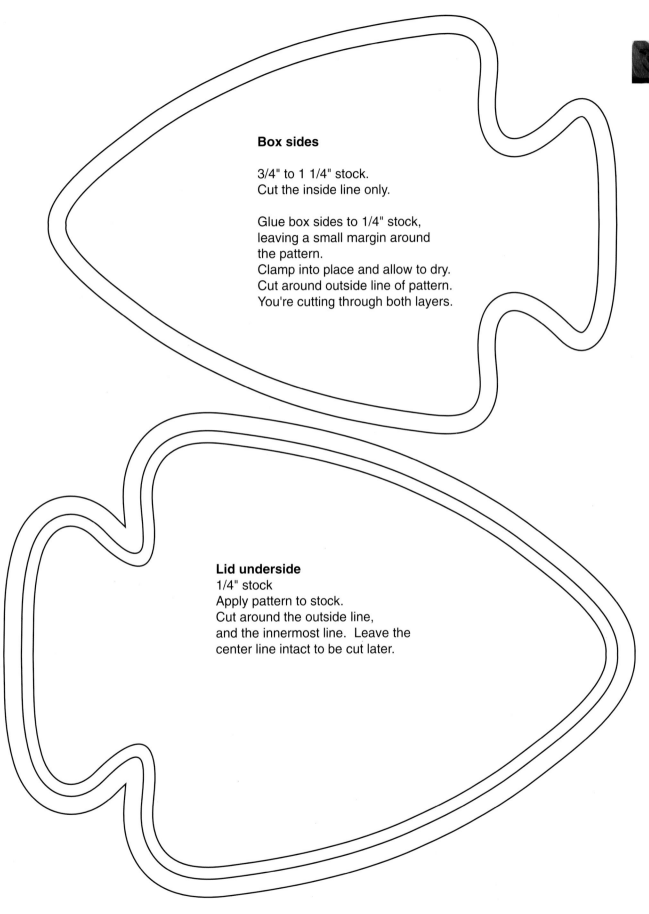

Box sides

3/4" to 1 1/4" stock.
Cut the inside line only.

Glue box sides to 1/4" stock,
leaving a small margin around
the pattern.
Clamp into place and allow to dry.
Cut around outside line of pattern.
You're cutting through both layers.

Lid underside
1/4" stock
Apply pattern to stock.
Cut around the outside line,
and the innermost line. Leave the
center line intact to be cut later.

WHIMSICAL HEART BOX

Overall dimensions:
$6^{1}/_{4}$" x $6^{1}/_{4}$" x $1^{1}/_{2}$"

Wood: Narra

This twist on a typical symmetrical heart makes an ideal keepsake box. Present it to the love of your life or a special family member.

#7 blade for cutting box sides
#5R blades for cutting lid

After box is assembled, round over lower
box edge and upper and lower lid edges
with a rotary tool fitted with a 1/8"
round over bit, or by hand with sandpaper.

Lid assembly
After cutting out both lid sections,
glue lid underside to lid upperside,
with pattern sides facing out.
Clamp into place and allow to dry.
Cut out around the center line of
the lid underside, cutting through both
thicknesses.

Lid upperside
1/4" stock
Apply the pattern to the stock.
Cut around the outside line.
Cut out all frets.

Box sides

3/4" to 1 1/4" stock.
Cut the inside line only.

Glue box sides to 1/4" stock,
leaving a small margin around
the pattern.
Clamp into place and allow to dry.
Cut around outside line of pattern.
You're cutting through both layers.

Lid underside
1/4" stock
Apply pattern to stock.
Cut around the outside line,
and the innermost line. Leave the
center line intact to be cut later.

TEARDROP BOX

Overall dimensions:
    4½" x 7½" x 1½"

Wood: Willow

Ordinary shapes, such as this teardrop, or comma, become beautiful boxes with the addition of scroll work.

#7 blade for cutting box sides
#5R blades for cutting lid

After box is assembled, round over lower
box edge and upper and lower lid edges
with a rotary tool fitted with a 1/8"
round over bit, or by hand with sandpaper.

Lid upper side
1/4" stock
Apply the pattern to the stock.
Cut around the outside line.
Cut out all frets.

Lid assembly
After cutting out both lid sections,
glue lid underside to lid upperside,
with pattern sides facing out.
Clamp into place and allow to dry.
Cut out around the center line of
the lid underside, cutting through both
thicknesses.

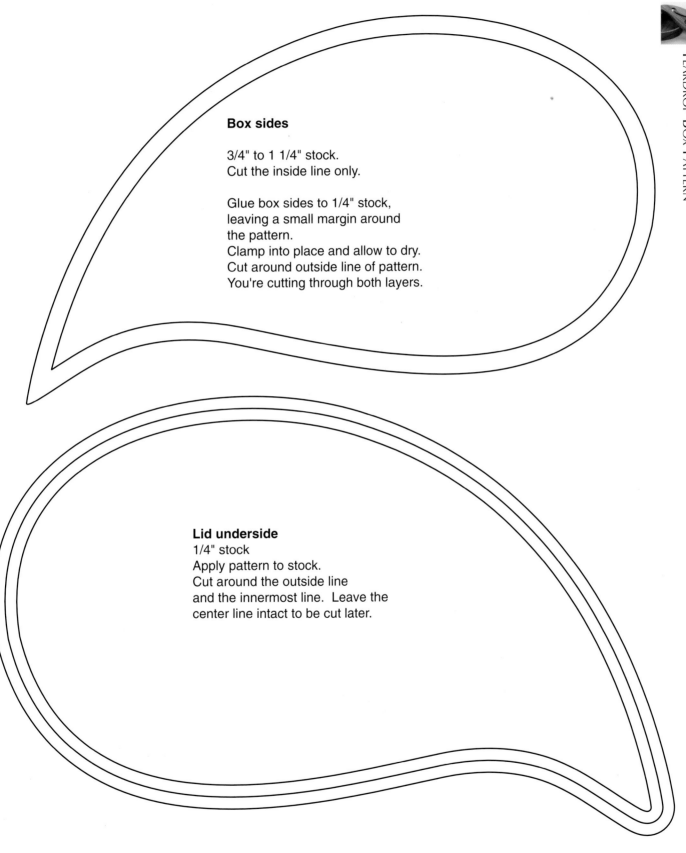

Box sides

3/4" to 1 1/4" stock.
Cut the inside line only.

Glue box sides to 1/4" stock,
leaving a small margin around
the pattern.
Clamp into place and allow to dry.
Cut around outside line of pattern.
You're cutting through both layers.

Lid underside
1/4" stock
Apply pattern to stock.
Cut around the outside line
and the innermost line. Leave the
center line intact to be cut later.

HOLY BIBLE BOX

Overall dimension:

   7" x 7" x 1½"

Wood: Genuine Mahogany

Provide a safe space for a personal or family
Bible with this upscale design of a square
box. The ribbon is cut with compound scroll
saw techniques.

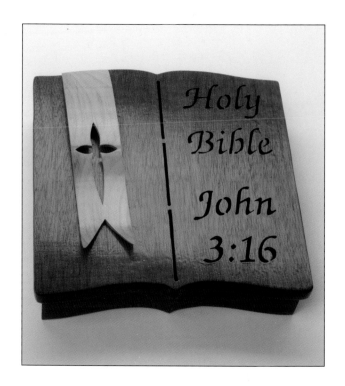

Lid assembly
After cutting out both lid sections,
glue lid underside to lid upperside,
with pattern sides facing out.
Clamp into place and allow to dry.
Cut out around the center line of
the lid underside, cutting through both
thicknesses.

#7 blade for cutting box sides
#5R blades for cutting lid
#5 blade for cutting bookmark
#3R blade for cutting letters
3/64 drill bit for stater holes in letters

After box is assembled, before bookmark
is glued into place, round over lower
box edge and upper and lower lid edges
with a rotary tool fitted with a 1/8"
round over bit, or by hand with sandpaper.

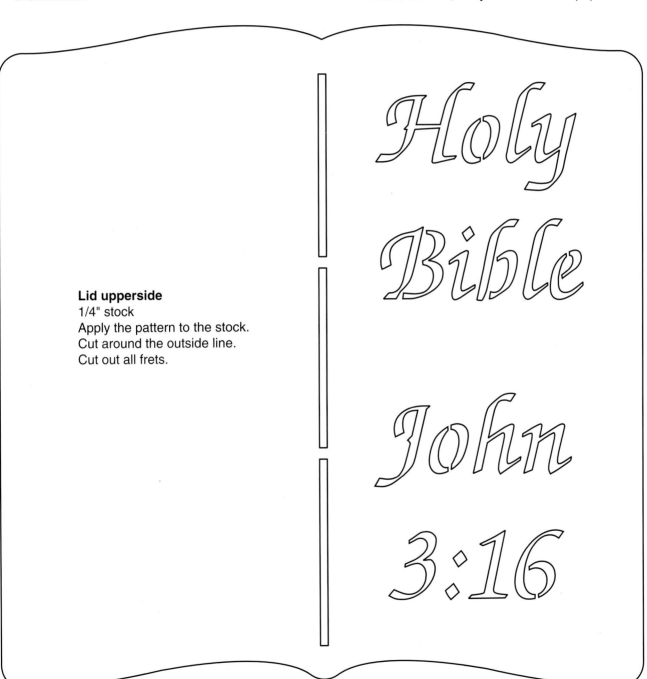

Lid upperside
1/4" stock
Apply the pattern to the stock.
Cut around the outside line.
Cut out all frets.

Box sides

3/4" to 1 1/4" stock.
Cut the inside line only.

Glue box sides to 1/4" stock,
leaving a small margin around
the pattern.
Clamp into place and allow to dry.
Cut around outside line of pattern.
You're cutting through both layers.

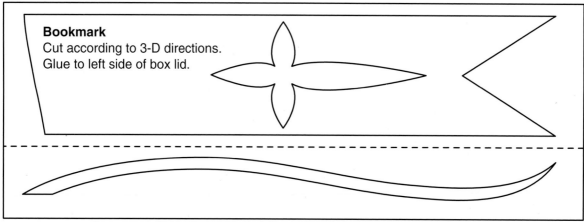

Bookmark
Cut according to 3-D directions.
Glue to left side of box lid.

Lid underside
1/4" stock
Apply pattern to stock.
Cut around the outside line
and the innermost line. Leave the
center line intact to be cut later.

POTPOURRI BOX

Overall dimensions:
    5³/₄" x 5³/₄" x 1¹/₂"

Wood: Butternut

An optional clear plastic top determines whether the contents of this box are for viewing or smelling.

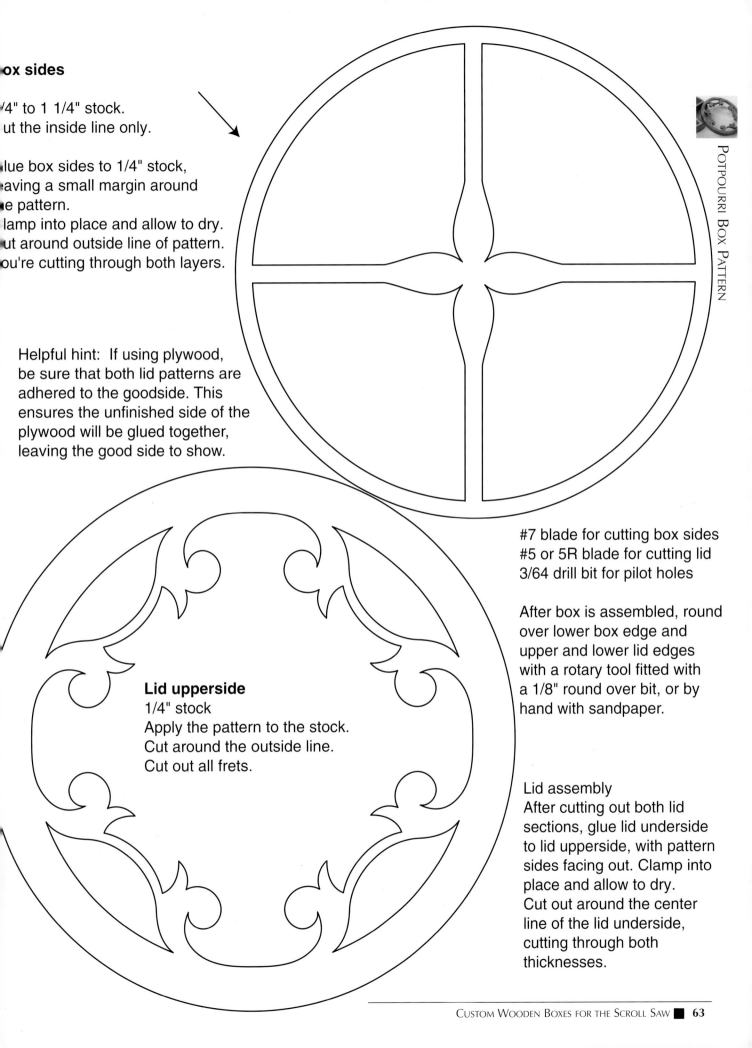

ox sides

/4" to 1 1/4" stock.
ut the inside line only.

lue box sides to 1/4" stock,
aving a small margin around
e pattern.
lamp into place and allow to dry.
ut around outside line of pattern.
ou're cutting through both layers.

Helpful hint: If using plywood,
be sure that both lid patterns are
adhered to the goodside. This
ensures the unfinished side of the
plywood will be glued together,
leaving the good side to show.

#7 blade for cutting box sides
#5 or 5R blade for cutting lid
3/64 drill bit for pilot holes

After box is assembled, round
over lower box edge and
upper and lower lid edges
with a rotary tool fitted with
a 1/8" round over bit, or by
hand with sandpaper.

Lid upperside
1/4" stock
Apply the pattern to the stock.
Cut around the outside line.
Cut out all frets.

Lid assembly
After cutting out both lid
sections, glue lid underside
to lid upperside, with pattern
sides facing out. Clamp into
place and allow to dry.
Cut out around the center
line of the lid underside,
cutting through both
thicknesses.

Lid underside
1/4" stock
Apply pattern to stock.
Cut around the outside line
and the innermost line. Leave the
center line intact to be cut later.

Plexiglass pattern
1/8" thickness

#12 blade
Leave the protective film on the plexiglass
as it is being cut.
Slow the saw speed down to at least half
to avoid having the plexiglass melt back
onto itself. If debris is not seen coming
from the kerf, the speed is too fast.

After box is totally assembled and the final
finish is applied, glue the plexiglass
to the lid underside.

Apply glue sparingly to the lid underside,
and set plexiglass into place

CIGAR BOX

Overall dimensions:
9" x 7¼" x 1½"

Wood: Sugar Pine and Birch plywood

A variation on a typical cigar box, this wooden container is a perfect fit for a handful of your favorite cigars.

Blade entry hole

Sawing direction

Cigars

Lid underside
1/4" stock
Apply pattern to stock.
Cut around the outside line
and the innermost line. Leave the
center line intact to be cut later.

#7 blade for cutting box sides
#5R blades for cutting lid
#3 blade for cutting letters and
lid relief.
3/64 drill bit for pilot holes

After box is assembled, round over lower
box edge and upper and lower lid edges
with a rotary tool fitted with a 1/8"
round over bit, or by hand with sandpaper.

Lid assembly
After cutting out both lid sections,
glue lid underside to lid upperside,
with pattern sides facing out.
Clamp into place and allow to dry.
Cut out around the center line of
the lid underside, cutting through both
thicknesses.

Lid upperside (pattern on opposite page)
1/4" stock
Apply the pattern to the stock.
Cut around the outside line.
Drill blade entry holes with a 3/64" bit.
Set saw table at 6 1/2 degrees, left side of table down.
Thread a #3 blade through the entry hole and cut around the figure,
sawing in the direction of the arrow.
If your saw table only tilts to the right, saw in the opposite direction
of the arrows.
Lay center relief aside to be glued in place after the lid is assembled.

Set the saw table back to zero!

Complete the lid as shown in the general directions.
Glue figures into place.
Mix a bit of glue with saw dust to fill in any holes left from the drill bit.

Box sides

3/4" to 1 1/4" stock.
Cut the inside line only.

Glue box sides to 1/4" stock,
leaving a small margin around
the pattern.
Clamp into place and allow to dry.
Cut around outside line of pattern.
You're cutting through both layers.

BUTTERFLY BOX

Overall dimensions:
    $7^3/4"$ x $5^3/4"$ x $1^1/2"$

Wood: Spanish Cedar

Consider flocking the interior or adding color to the scrolled cutouts on the lid of this shapely box.

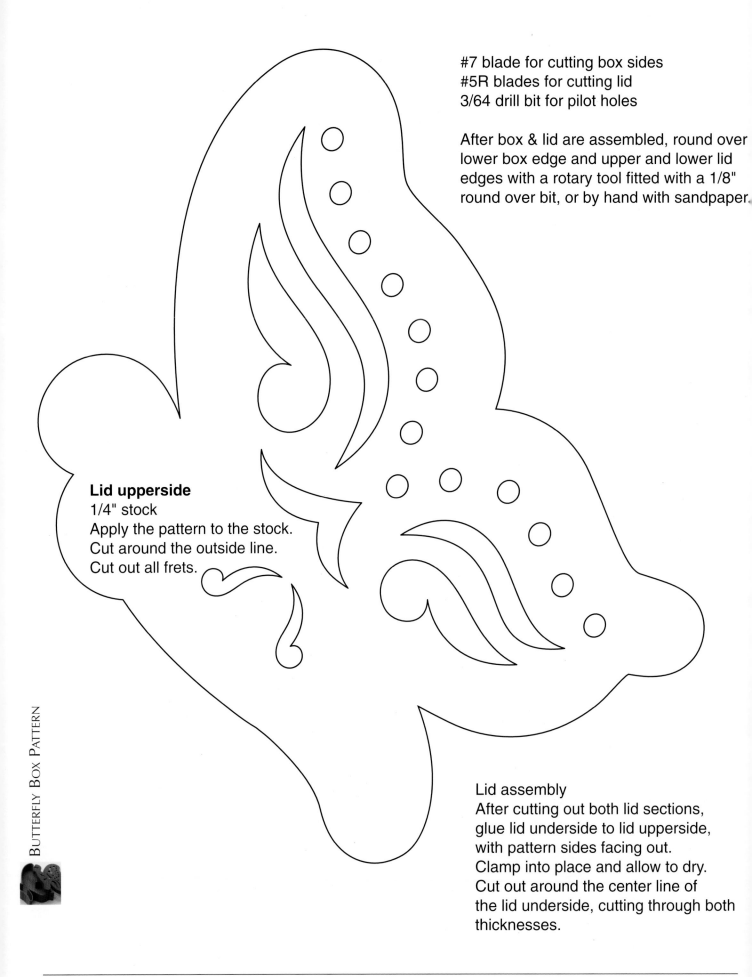

#7 blade for cutting box sides
#5R blades for cutting lid
3/64 drill bit for pilot holes

After box & lid are assembled, round over lower box edge and upper and lower lid edges with a rotary tool fitted with a 1/8" round over bit, or by hand with sandpaper.

Lid upperside
1/4" stock
Apply the pattern to the stock.
Cut around the outside line.
Cut out all frets.

Lid assembly
After cutting out both lid sections, glue lid underside to lid upperside, with pattern sides facing out.
Clamp into place and allow to dry.
Cut out around the center line of the lid underside, cutting through both thicknesses.

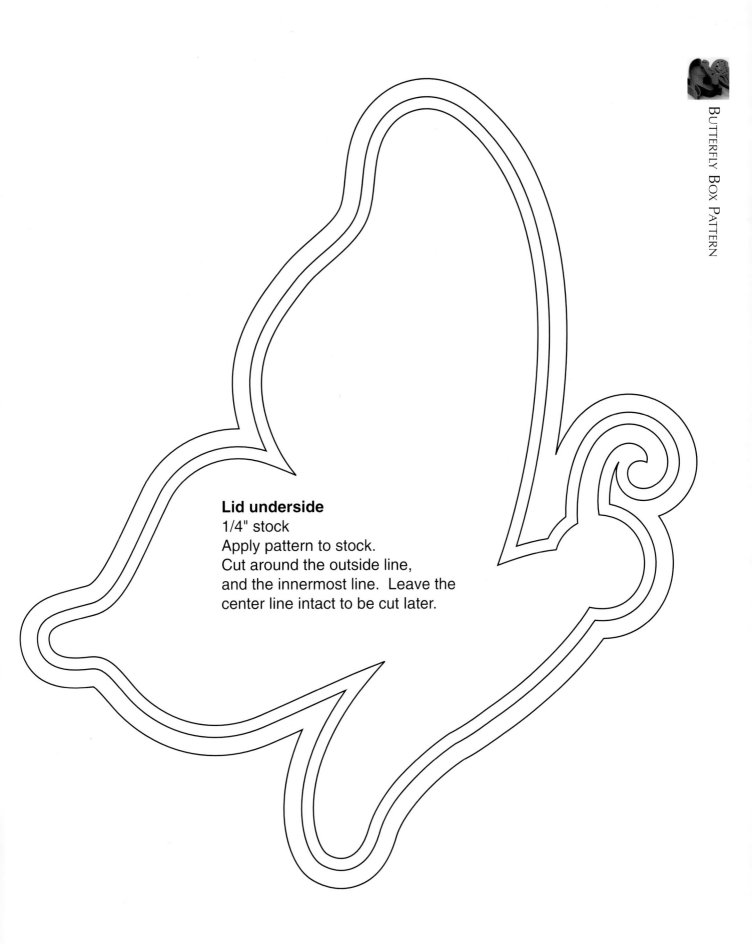

Lid underside
1/4" stock
Apply pattern to stock.
Cut around the outside line,
and the innermost line. Leave the
center line intact to be cut later.

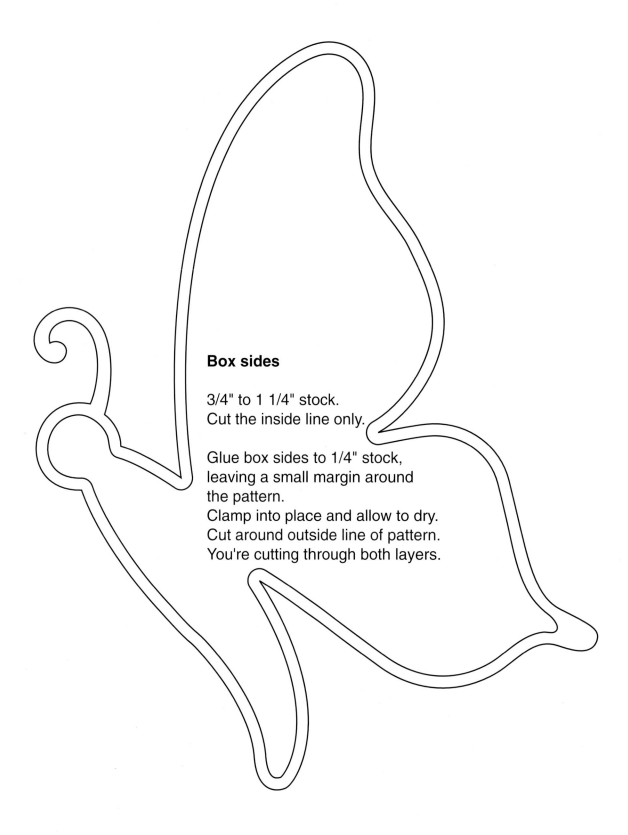

Box sides

3/4" to 1 1/4" stock.
Cut the inside line only.

Glue box sides to 1/4" stock,
leaving a small margin around
the pattern.
Clamp into place and allow to dry.
Cut around outside line of pattern.
You're cutting through both layers.

Harp Box

Overall dimensions:
5$\frac{7}{8}$" x 9$\frac{3}{8}$" x 1$\frac{1}{2}$"

Wood: Canary Wood

Keepsake boxes that remind the owner of his or her hobby or special interest are sure to please. Add initials for additional personalization.

Lid assembly
After cutting out both lid sections, glue lid underside to lid upperside, with pattern sides facing out. Clamp into place and allow to dry. Cut out around the center line of the lid underside, cutting through both thicknesses.

#7 blade for cutting box sides
#5R blades for cutting lid
#3R blade for cutting letters
3/64 drill bit for pilot holes

After box & lid are assembled, round over lower box edge and upper and lower lid edges with a rotary tool fitted with a 1/8" round over bit, or by hand with sandpaper.

Lid upperside
1/4" stock
Apply the pattern to the stock.
Cut around the outside line.
Cut out all frets.

HARP BOX PATTERN

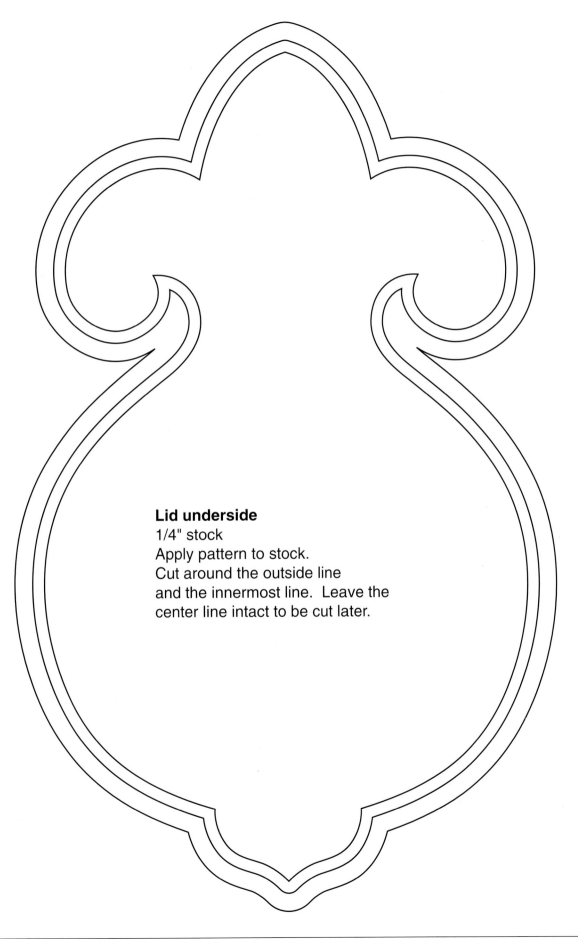

Lid underside
1/4" stock
Apply pattern to stock.
Cut around the outside line
and the innermost line. Leave the
center line intact to be cut later.

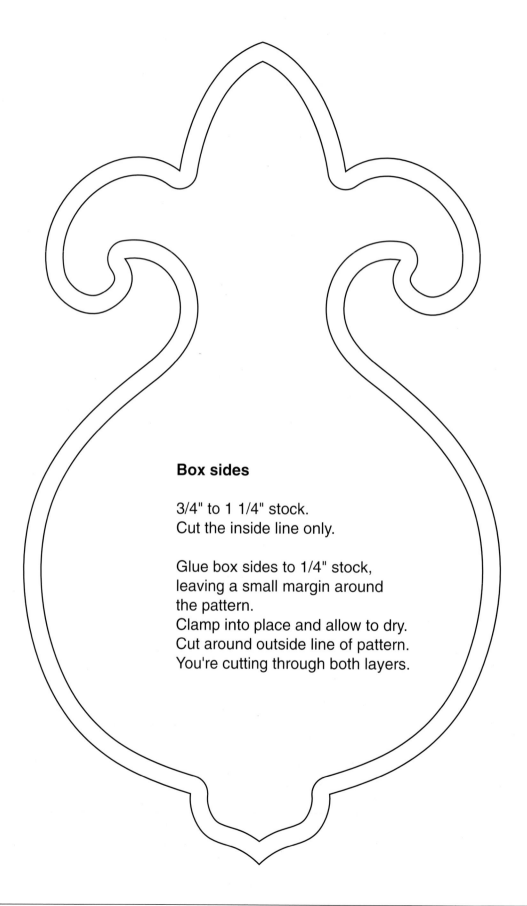

Box sides

3/4" to 1 1/4" stock.
Cut the inside line only.

Glue box sides to 1/4" stock,
leaving a small margin around
the pattern.
Clamp into place and allow to dry.
Cut around outside line of pattern.
You're cutting through both layers.

KALEIDOSCOPE BOX

Overall dimensions:
7¼" x 7¼" x 1½"

Wood: Genuine Mahogany

Nothing states that boxes have to be square. Experiment with other shapes, like this octagon. The compound handle makes it easy to lift this otherwise potentially awkward-to-remove lid.

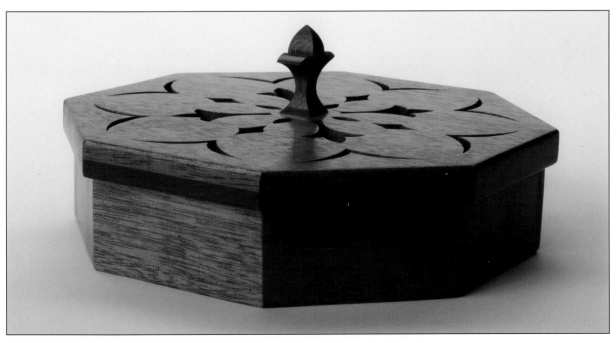

Lid top
1/4" stock
Apply the pattern to the stock.
Cut around the outside line.
Cut out all frets.

Lid assembly
After cutting out both lid sections,
glue lid underside to lid upperside,
with pattern sides facing out.
Clamp into place and allow to dry.
Cut out around the center line of
the lid underside, cutting through both
thicknesses.

#7 blade for cutting box sides
#5R blades for cutting lid
#5 blade for cutting handle

After box is assembled, before handle
is glued into place, round over lower
box edge and upper and lower lid edges
with a rotary tool fitted with a 1/8"
round over bit, or by hand with sandpaper.

Box sides

3/4" to 1 1/4" stock.
Cut the inside line only.

Glue box sides to 1/4" stock,
leaving a small margin around
the pattern.
Clamp into place and allow to dry.
Cut around outside line of pattern.
You're cutting through both layers.

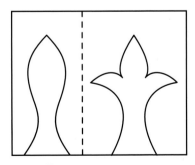

Handle
Cut 1 according to 3-D directions.
Glue handle to center of lid.

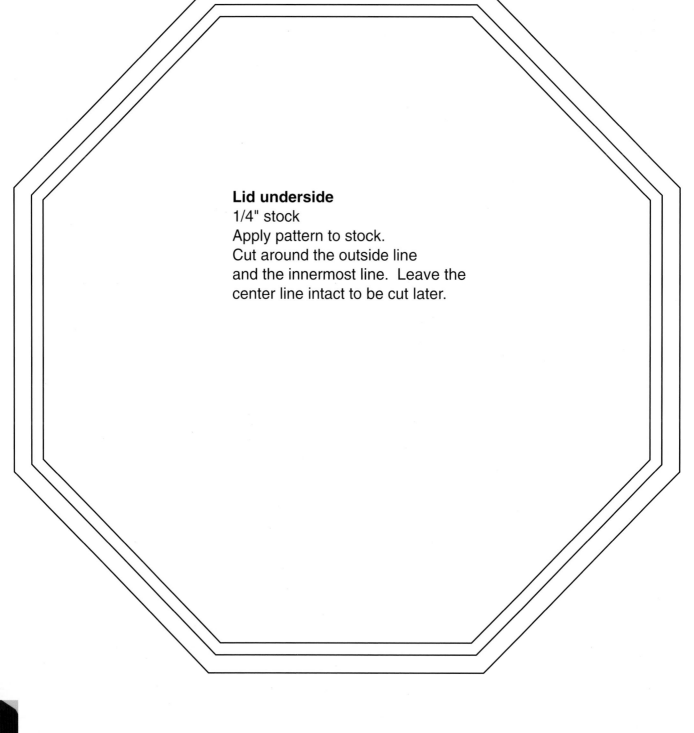

Lid underside
1/4" stock
Apply pattern to stock.
Cut around the outside line
and the innermost line. Leave the
center line intact to be cut later.

SCALLOPED OVAL BOX

Overall dimensions:
   7³/4" x 5¹/2" x 1¹/2"

Wood: Red Cedar

Add beauty and elegance to any box by scalloping the edges. Other options for decorating boxes include compound-cut handles and raised platforms.

Lid riser
1/4" stock
Cut 1

#7 blades for cutting box sides
#5R blades for cutting all other pieces
#5 blade for cutting handle

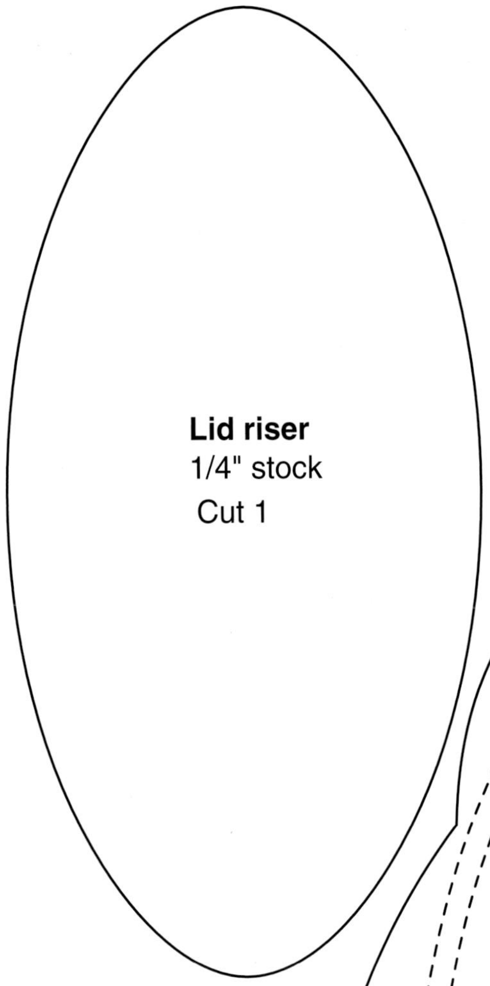

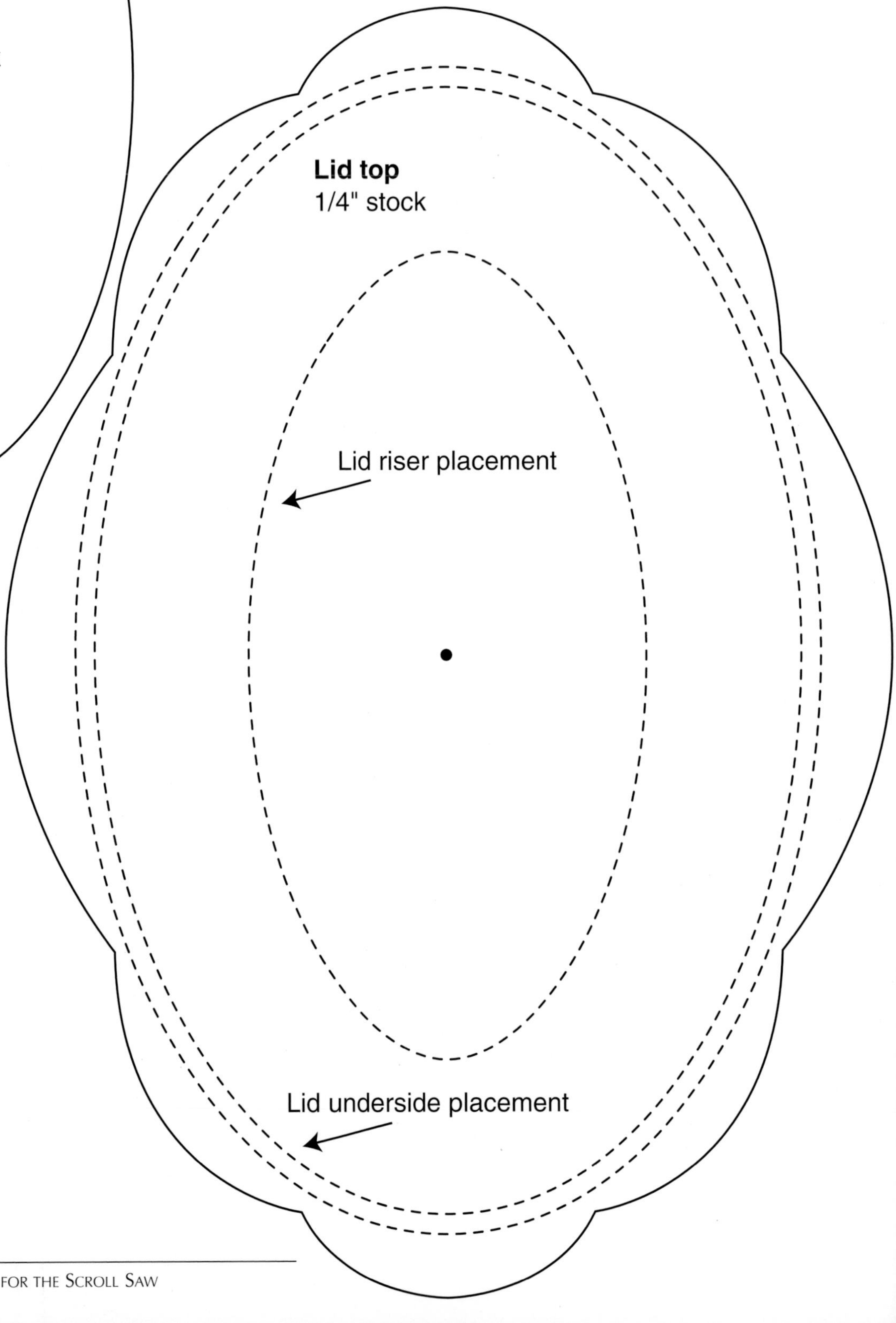

Lid top
1/4" stock

Lid riser placement

Lid underside placement

SCALLOPED OVAL BOX PATTERN

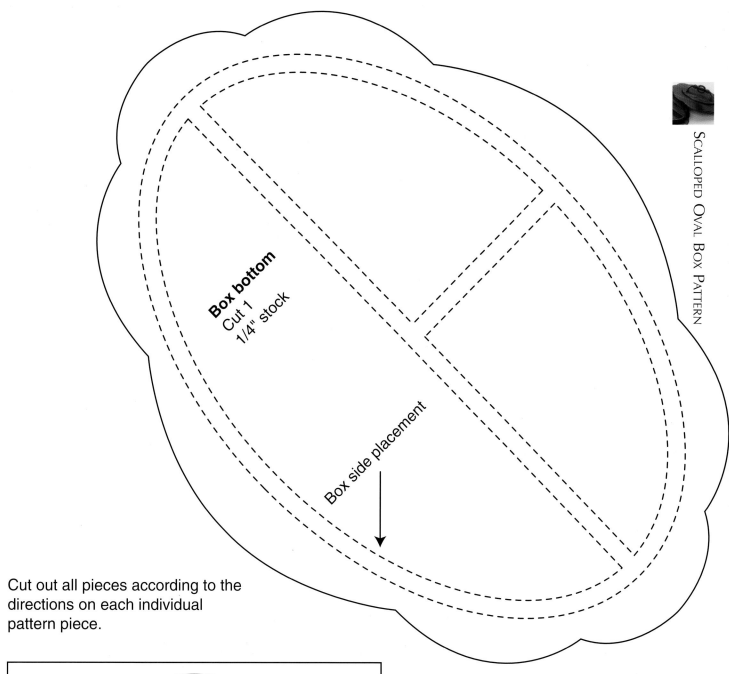

Box bottom
Cut 1
1/4" stock

Box side placement

Cut out all pieces according to the
directions on each individual
pattern piece.

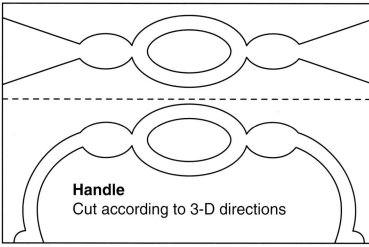

Handle
Cut according to 3-D directions

With a 1/8" round over bit installed
in a rotary tool, round over both
edges of the lid and base pieces, or
round over edges with sandpaper.
Round over only the outside edge
of the lid underside and the lid riser.

Glue the unrouted side of the lid
underside to the underside of the lid,
making sure it is centered. Glue the
unrouted side of the lid riser to the top
side of the lid, making sure it is centered.
Glue the handle to the center of the lid riser.
Glue the box side to the box bottom.

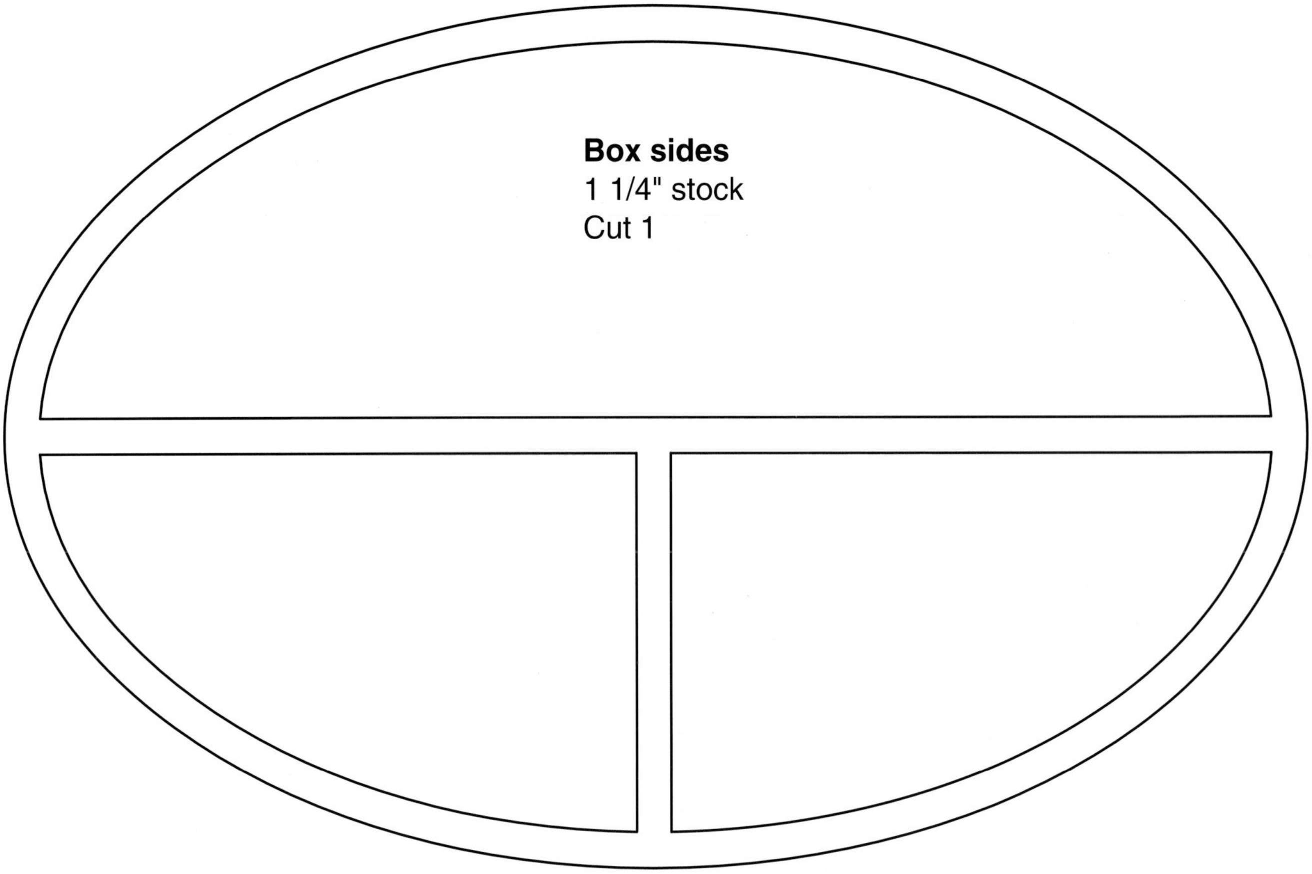

Box sides
1 1/4" stock
Cut 1

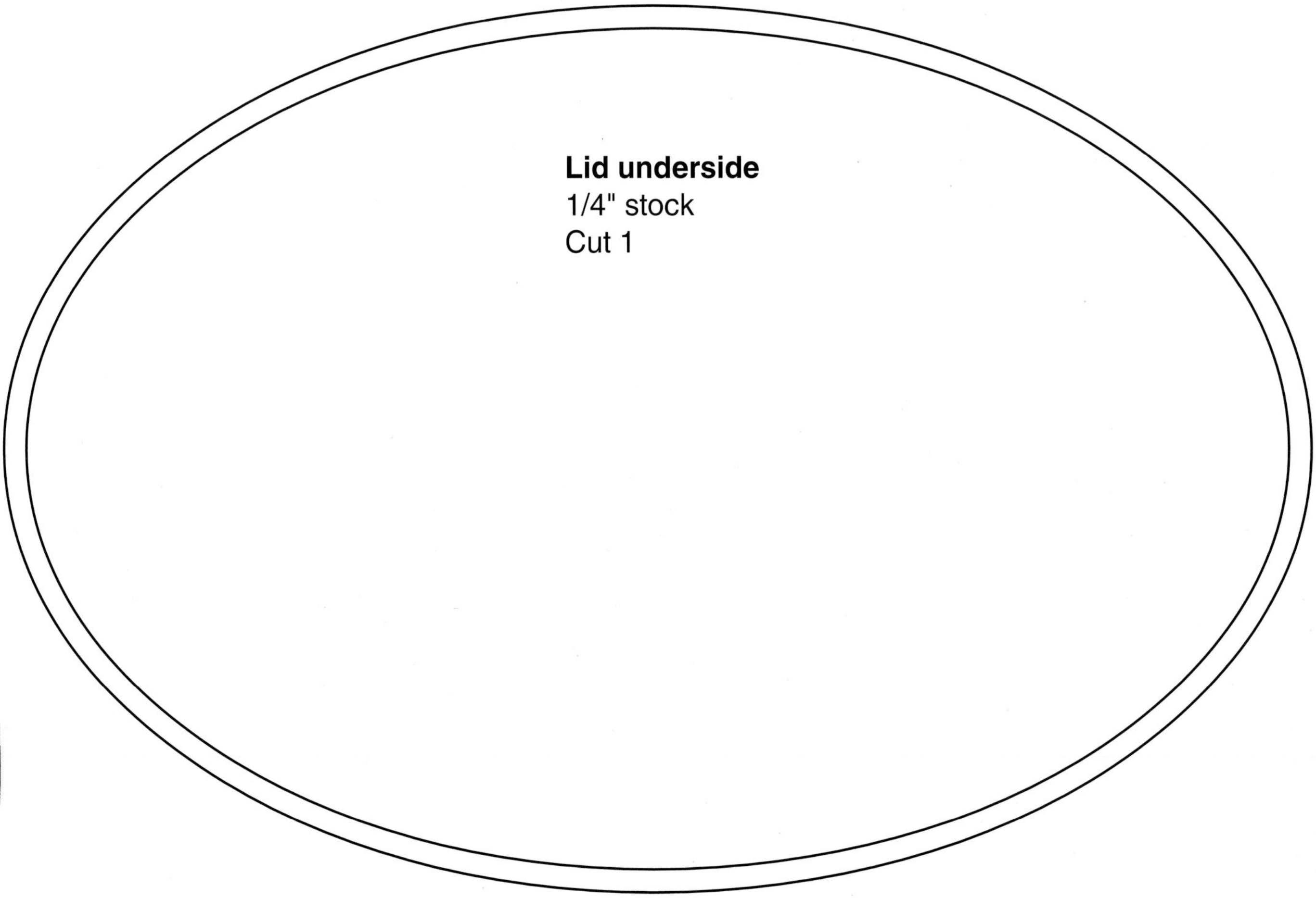

Lid underside
1/4" stock
Cut 1

SCROLL BOX

Overall dimensions:
 8¹/₄" x 5¹/₄" x 1¹/₂"

Wood: Lacewood

Make the most of woods with interesting grain by toning down or eliminating the scrollwork on the lid. Here, these simple lines do not compete with the unusual grain pattern.

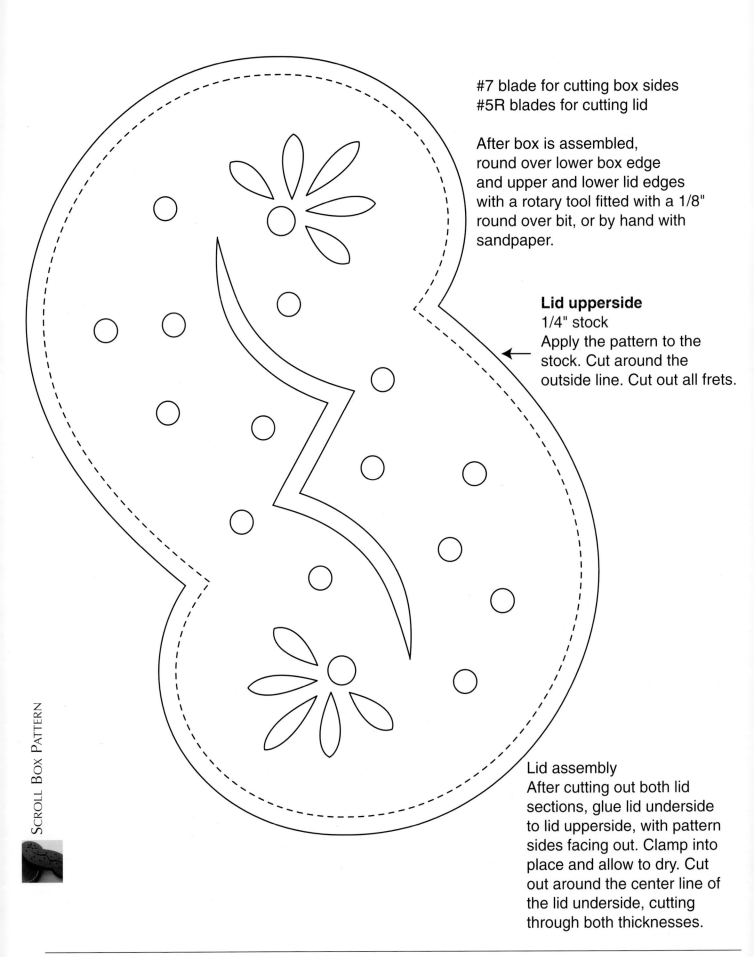

#7 blade for cutting box sides
#5R blades for cutting lid

After box is assembled,
round over lower box edge
and upper and lower lid edges
with a rotary tool fitted with a 1/8"
round over bit, or by hand with
sandpaper.

Lid upperside
1/4" stock
Apply the pattern to the
stock. Cut around the
outside line. Cut out all frets.

Lid assembly
After cutting out both lid
sections, glue lid underside
to lid upperside, with pattern
sides facing out. Clamp into
place and allow to dry. Cut
out around the center line of
the lid underside, cutting
through both thicknesses.

SCROLL BOX PATTERN

Box sides

3/4" to 1 1/4" stock.
Cut the inside line only.

Glue box sides to 1/4" stock,
leaving a small margin around
the pattern.
Clamp into place and allow to dry.
Cut around outside line of pattern.
You're cutting through both layers.

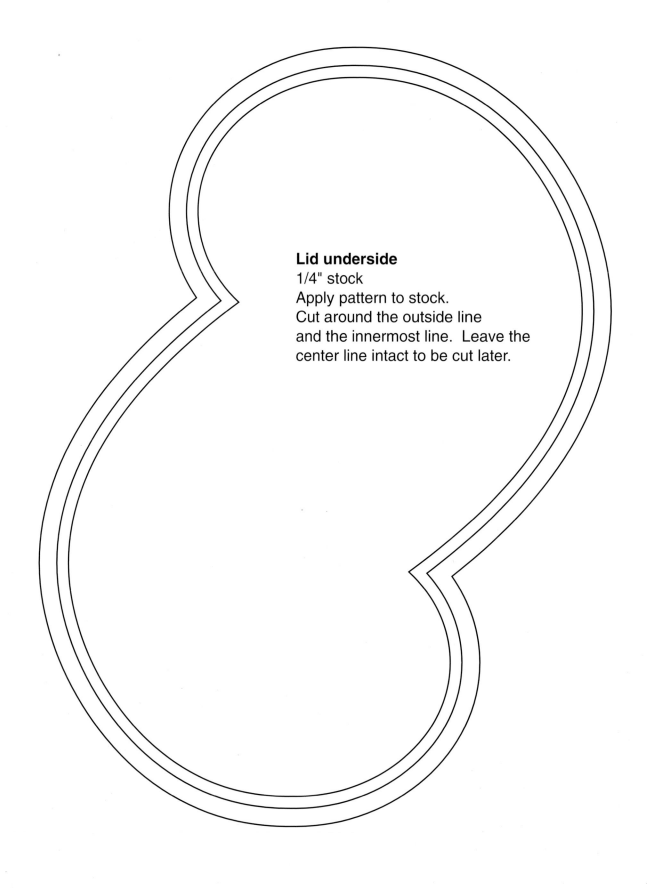

Lid underside
1/4" stock
Apply pattern to stock.
Cut around the outside line
and the innermost line. Leave the
center line intact to be cut later.

ACE OF SPADES BOX

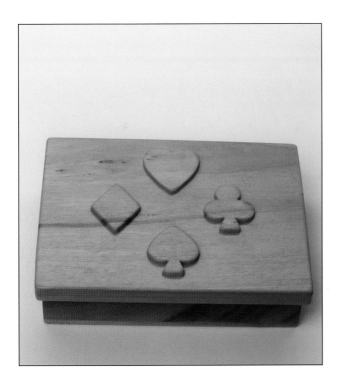

Overall dimensions:
    6³/4" x 5" x ¹/2"

Wood: Willow

Making inside cuts while the saw table is slightly tilted creates scrolled frets that push almost, but not quite, all the way out of the lid.

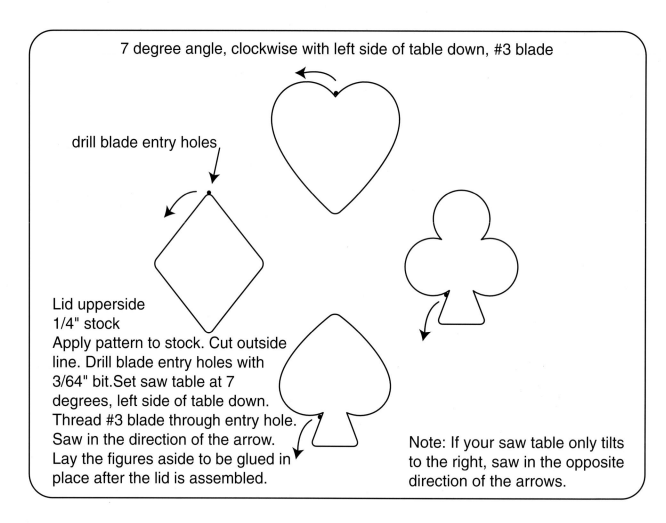

7 degree angle, clockwise with left side of table down, #3 blade

drill blade entry holes

Lid upperside
1/4" stock
Apply pattern to stock. Cut outside
line. Drill blade entry holes with
3/64" bit.Set saw table at 7
degrees, left side of table down.
Thread #3 blade through entry hole.
Saw in the direction of the arrow.
Lay the figures aside to be glued in
place after the lid is assembled.

Note: If your saw table only tilts
to the right, saw in the opposite
direction of the arrows.

Set the saw table back to zero!
Finish cutting the lid underside and
the box sides.Glue figures into place.
Mix a bit of glue with saw dust to fill in any
holes left from the drill bit.

ACE OF SPADES BOX PATTERN

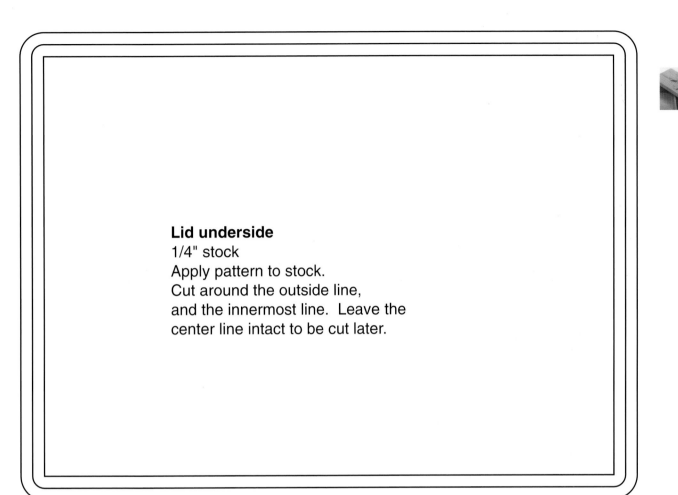

Lid underside
1/4" stock
Apply pattern to stock.
Cut around the outside line,
and the innermost line. Leave the
center line intact to be cut later.

Box sides

3/4" to 1 1/4" stock
Apply pattern to stock.
Cut the inside lines only.

Glue box sides to 1/4" stock,
leaving a small margin around
the pattern.
Clamp into place and allow to dry.
Cut around outside lines of pattern.

Double Heart Box

Overall dimensions:
    6$\frac{1}{2}$" x 5" x 1$\frac{1}{2}$"

Wood: Alder

Personalize any wooden box with names and dates of special occasions. Notice how the line separating the hearts remains as a divider for the interior space of the box.

#7 blade for cutting box sides
#5R blades for cutting lid
#3 blade for cutting letters
3/64 drill bit for pilot holes

After box is assembled, round over lower
box edge and upper and lower lid edges
with a rotary tool fitted with a 1/8"
round over bit, or by hand with sandpaper.

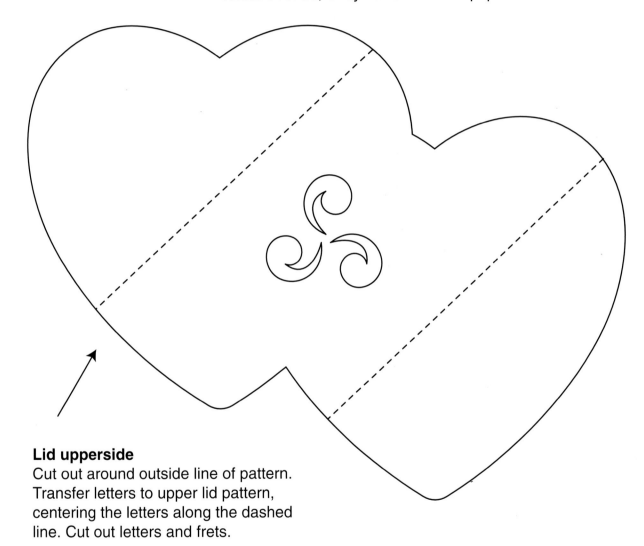

Lid upperside
Cut out around outside line of pattern.
Transfer letters to upper lid pattern,
centering the letters along the dashed
line. Cut out letters and frets.

Helpful hint: If using plywood, be sure that
both lid patterns are adhered to the good
side. This insures the unfinished side of the
plywood will be glued together, leaving the
good side to show.

Box sides

3/4" to 1 1/4" stock (thickness of choice). Apply pattern to stock. Cut the inside lines only.

Glue box sides to 1/4" stock, leaving a small margin around the pattern.
Clamp into place and allow to dry.
Cut around outside lines of pattern.

Lid underside
1/4" stock
Apply pattern to stock.
Cut around the outside line, and the innermost line. Leave the center line intact to be cut later.

GRAPE LEAF BOX

Overall dimensions:
    8$\frac{1}{2}$" x 6" x 1$\frac{1}{2}$"

Wood: Poplar

A painted motif, such as this bunch of grapes, can add color and interest to any box. The grapes, leaves and stems were glued directly to the lid.

#7 blade for cutting box sides
#5R blades for cutting lid
#5 blade for cutting leaves

After box is assembled, before grapes
and leaves are glued into place,
round over lower box edge and upper
and lower lid edges with a rotary tool fitted
with a 1/8" round over bit, or by hand
with sandpaper.

To make grapes.
Cut in half eight, 1/2" round wooden
balls. If desired, add a hint of color with
watered down acrylic craft paint.

Lid underside
1/4" stock
Apply pattern to stock,
and cut the inside lines only.
Glue lid underside to 1/4" stock,
leaving a small margin around
the pattern.
Clamp into place and allow to dry.
Cut around outside lines of pattern.

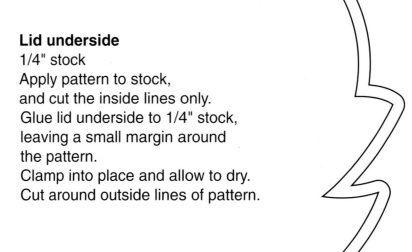

Placement diagram

GRAPE LEAF BOX PATTERN

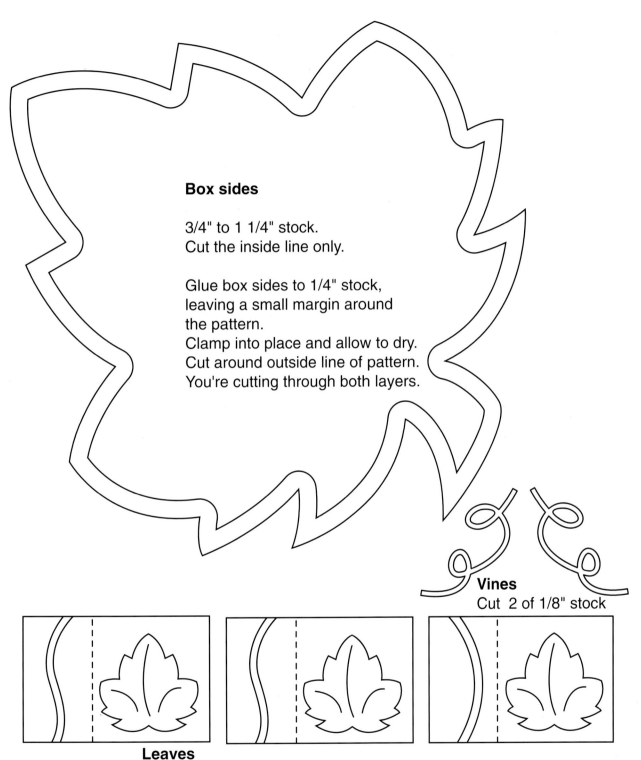

Box sides

3/4" to 1 1/4" stock.
Cut the inside line only.

Glue box sides to 1/4" stock,
leaving a small margin around
the pattern.
Clamp into place and allow to dry.
Cut around outside line of pattern.
You're cutting through both layers.

Vines
Cut 2 of 1/8" stock

Leaves
Cut 1 of each using 3-D cutting techniques

DOGWOOD BOX

Overall dimensions:
4½" x 4½" x 1½"

Wood: Black Walnut with Magnolia accents

Cut compound elements, such as this dogwood flower in contrasting wood. Here the light color of the dogwood flower is captured in magnolia wood.

Lid underside

1/4" stock
Apply pattern to stock,
and cut the inside lines only.

Glue lid underside to 1/4" stock,
leaving a small margin around
the pattern.
Clamp into place and allow to dry.
Cut around outside lines of pattern.

Glue petals and leaves to assembled lid
according to diagram.

Leaves

Cut 2 of 1/8" stock

#7 blade for cutting box sides
#5R blades for cutting lid
#5 blade for cutting blossom

After box is assembled, before blossom is
glued into place, round over lower
box edge and upper and lower lid edges
with a rotary tool fitted with a 1/8"
round over bit, or by hand with sandpaper.

Box sides

3/4" to 1 1/4" stock.
Cut the inside line only.

Glue box sides to 1/4" stock,
leaving a small margin around
the pattern.
Clamp into place and allow to dry.
Cut around outside line of pattern.
You're cutting through both layers.

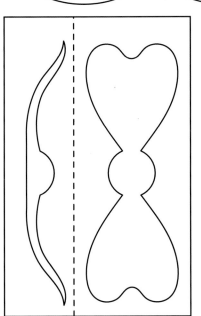

Petal 1 Cut 1

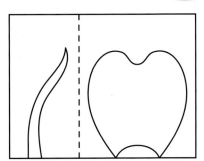

Petal 2 Cut 2 using 3-D techniques

Blossom placement diagram

SUNBONNET SUE BOX

Overall dimensions:
$5^1/4"$ x 8" x $1^1/2"$

Wood: Sugar Pine and Birch plywood

Inexpensive wood can be painted with bright
acrylic paints in familiar patterns to make
attractive keepsake boxes. This box design
was adapted from a popular quilt block.

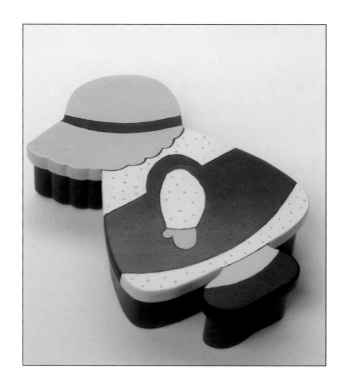

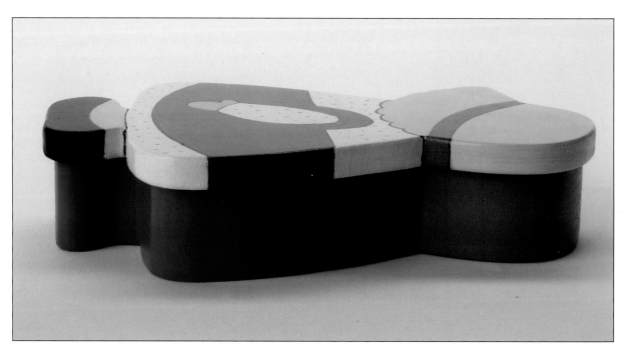

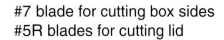

#7 blade for cutting box sides
#5R blades for cutting lid

After box is assembled, round over lower box edge and upper and lower lid edges with a rotary tool fitted with a 1/8" round over bit, or by hand with sandpaper.

Lid underside
1/4" stock
Apply pattern to stock,
and cut the inside lines only.
Glue lid underside to 1/4" stock,
leaving a small margin around
the pattern.
Clamp into place and allow to dry.
Cut around outside lines of pattern.

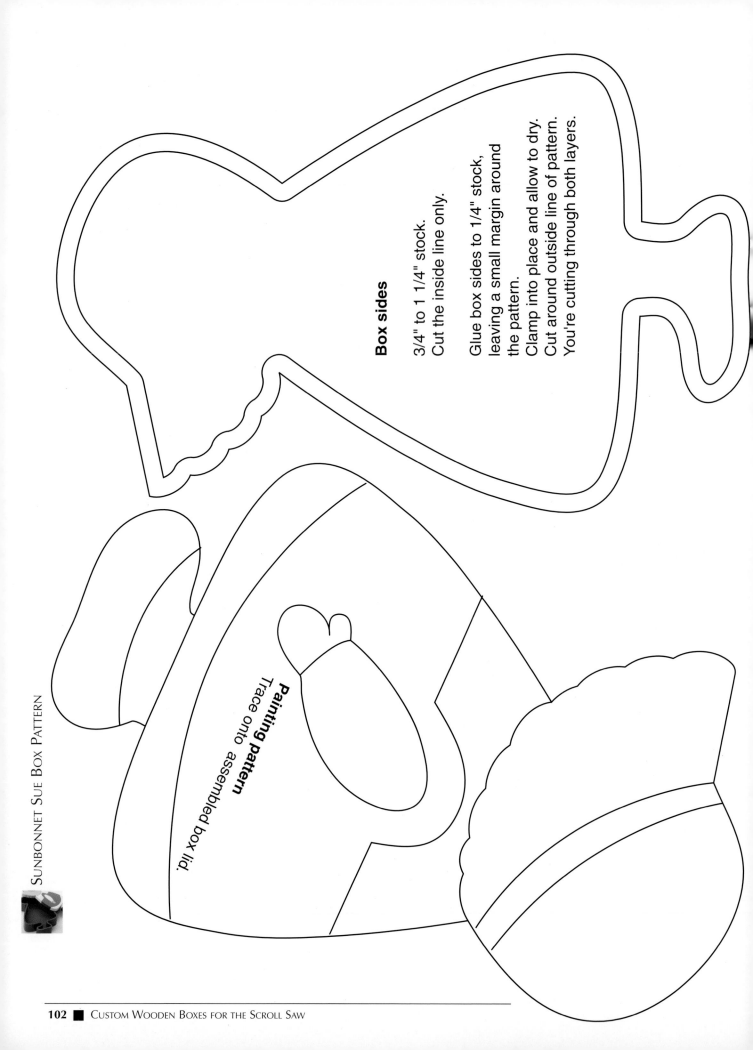

SUNBONNET SUE BOX PATTERN

Box sides

3/4" to 1 1/4" stock.
Cut the inside line only.

Glue box sides to 1/4" stock, leaving a small margin around the pattern.
Clamp into place and allow to dry.
Cut around outside line of pattern.
You're cutting through both layers.

Painting pattern
Trace onto assembled box lid.

CLASSIC ROUND BOX

Overall dimensions:
    5" x 5" x 1½"

Wood: Cypress with Black Walnut

Leave the lid of this box uncut or use inlay (top) or relief (bottom) cutting techniques to create a distinctive lid. Try your hand at creating other simple designs such as dolphins, stars and stylized flowers to fit within the dimensions of this lid.

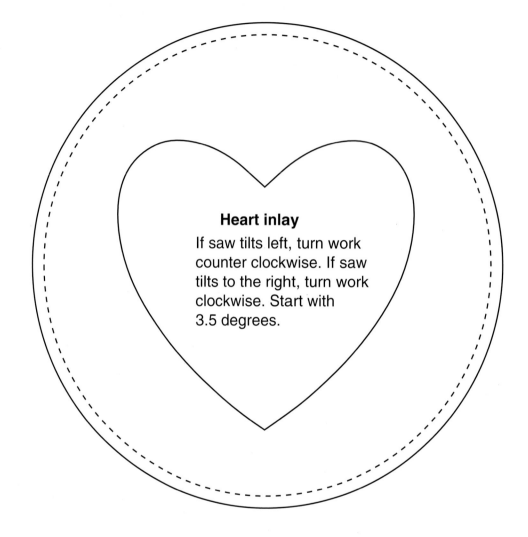

Heart inlay

If saw tilts left, turn work counter clockwise. If saw tilts to the right, turn work clockwise. Start with 3.5 degrees.

Box sides

3/4" to 1 1/4" stock.
Cut the inside line only.

Glue box sides to 1/4" stock,
leaving a small margin around
the pattern.
Clamp into place and allow to dry.
Cut around outside line of pattern.
You're cutting through both layers.

Lid underside
1/4" stock
Apply pattern to stock.
Cut around the outside line,
and the innermost line. Leave the
center line intact to be cut later.

Classic Oval Box

Overall dimensions:

6½" x 4⅞" x 1½"

Wood: Sugar Pine and Birch plywood

Experiment with a variety of finishing techniques, especially when the box is cut from pine or plywood. Here, a decoupage finish (watered down glue and wrapping paper) creates a classy look on an otherwise plain box.

Box sides

3/4" to 1 1/4" stock.
Cut the inside line only.

Glue box sides to 1/4" stock,
leaving a small margin around
the pattern.
Clamp into place and allow to dry.
Cut around outside line of pattern.
You're cutting through both layers.

After box is assembled,
round over lower box edge
and upper and lower lid edges
with a rotary tool fitted with a 1/8"
round over bit, or by hand
with sandpaper.

#7 blade for cutting box sides
#5R blades for cutting lid

Lid underside
1/4" stock
Apply pattern to stock,
and cut the inside lines only.
Glue lid underside to 1/4" stock,
leaving a small margin around
the pattern.
Clamp into place and allow to dry.
Cut around outside lines of pattern.

More Great Project Books from Fox Chapel Publishing

• **A Woodworker's Guide to Making Traditional Mirrors and Picture Frames by John A. Nelson:** A sourcebook of patterns for woodworkers that features plans for mirrors and frames. Learn the basics behind cutting wood for mirrors and frames, and then use the included measured drawings to create your own.
ISBN: 1-56523-223-2, 112 pages, soft cover, $17.95.

• **Scroll Saw Workbook 2nd Edition by John A. Nelson:** The ultimate beginner's scrolling guide! Hone your scroll saw skills to perfection with the 25 skill-building chapters and projects included in this book. Techniques and patterns for wood and non-wood projects!
ISBN: 1-56523-207-0, 88 pages, soft cover, $14.95.

• **Intarsia Workbook by Judy Gale Roberts:** Learn the art of intarsia from the #1 expert, Judy Gale Roberts! You'll be amazed at the beautiful pictures you can create when you learn to combine different colors and textures of wood to make raised 3-D images. It features 7 projects and expert instructions. Great for beginners!
ISBN: 1-56523-226-7, 72 pages, soft cover, $14.95.

• **Wooden Chess Sets You Can Make by Diana Thompson:** Handcraft a classic or contemporary chess set that will be cherished for years to come. You will learn to create each piece by using compound cuts on the scroll saw. Patterns and full-color photographs for each of the playing pieces (king, queen, bishop, knight, rook, and pawn) are included. Instructions and pattern for a beautiful inlay playing board also included.
ISBN: 1-56523-188-0, 72 pages, soft cover, $14.95.

• **3-D Patterns for the Scroll Saw by Diana Thompson:** Learn the basics of compound scrolling through step-by-step demonstrations, helpful hints, and time-saving techniques. Features 45 shop-tested and ready-to-use patterns!
ISBN: 1-56523-158-9, 64 pages, soft cover, $14.95.

• **Compound Christmas Ornaments for the Scroll Saw by Diana Thompson:** Start your holiday scrolling with the 57 festive projects in this book! Ornaments, nativity scene, tree topper, holiday centerpieces, snowmen candlestick holders, and much more!
ISBN: 1-56523-181-3, 72 pages, soft cover, $14.95.

• **Compound Scroll Saw Creations by Diana Thompson:** Cut compound clocks, candlestick holders and characters on your scroll saw. It includes shop-tested patterns, basic instructions and information on wood choices.
ISBN: 1-56523-170-8, 72 pages, soft cover, $14.95.

• **Complete Guide to Making Wooden Clocks, 2nd Edition by John A. Nelson:** Never run out of ideas for clocks again! John Nelson offers plans and parts lists for a wide variety of traditional, Shaker, and contemporary clocks. Features 37 projects, a review of clock components, an inside look at the history of clock-making in America, and beautiful photographs of America's favorite clocks.
ISBN: 1-56523-208-9, 184 pages, soft cover, $19.95.

• **Making Doll Furniture in Wood by Dennis Simmons:** Learn to make hand-made doll furniture with the 30 projects featured in this book! Inside you will find 5 step-by-step projects for bed, dresser, chair and more. You'll also find measured drawings for an additional 25 pieces of furniture. Projects are perfectly sized for American Girl® or any other 18" doll.
ISBN: 1-56523-200-3, 120 pages, soft cover, $19.95.

• **Scroll Saw Holiday Puzzles by Tony and June Burns:** You'll be scrolling throughout the year with this festive collection of scroll saw puzzles for the holidays! From New Year's Eve and Christmas to Valentine's Day, Easter, and Halloween, you'll find over 25 delightful puzzle patterns for over 15 holidays and seasons. Basic scrolling information such as choosing a blade, safety and tips also included!
ISBN: 1-56523-204-6, 72 pages, soft cover, $14.95.

CHECK WITH YOUR LOCAL WOODWORKING STORE OR BOOK RETAILER
Or call 800-457-9112 • Visit www.foxchapelpublishing.com